LANDMARKS IN LITERATURE

Maynard Mack, *Series Editor*
Yale University

Some books belong to all times and places. They are the rivers, mountains, seas, and continents of our intellectual and moral world. They tell us where we are and how far we have still to go. They are, in short, our landmarks.

Landmarks in Literature is a series of interpretive studies of such books, each written by an authority of today, each a reference point between our present and our past.

EDWARD B. IRVING, JR., author of this volume in the Landmarks in Literature series, is Associate Professor of English at the University of Pennsylvania. He is the editor of *The Old English "Exodus"* and is the author of *A Reading of "Beowulf"* and various articles on Old English literature.

ANGLO-SAXON ENGLAND

Showing Places Mentioned in the Text

THE SETTING OF *BEOWULF*

(Locations of tribes are necessarily vague.)

0°   4°   20°

SWEDES

GEATS

60°

North
Sea

56°

(JUTES)

DANES

Heorot?

Baltic Sea

(ANGLES)

HEATHOBARDS?
(SAXONS)

BRITAIN

FRISIANS

FRANKS

0   50   100   150

miles

CHOICE   MAR. '70

Language & Literature

English & American

IRVING, Edward B., Jr. **Introduction to Beowulf.** **Prentice-Hall, 1969.**
    112p map bibl 77-79447. 3.95
The best description of this volume is the author's: "too much for some
and too little or too elementary for others." A great many facts are
indeed presented in this attempt to anticipate questions asked by undergraduates, facts for which one would have to turn to R. W. Chambers'
Beowulf: An Introduction (1921), or to volumes like D. Whitelock's
The Audience of Beowulf (1951), or even to Garmonsway and Simpson's
Beowulf and Its Analogues (1969). But there remains an artificial,
popularizing tone to these facts, supported as they are by maps, chrono-
logical charts, and summaries. In spite of this unfortunate tone, particularly offensive in the imaginary scenes introducing the work, Irving's
Introduction does fill a gap between the specialist and the neophyte.
Recommended for undergraduate collections — and for graduate students cramming for general examinations.

INTRODUCTION

TO

BEOWULF

❦ ❧

EDWARD B. IRVING, JR.

PRENTICE-HALL, INC., ENGLEWOOD CLIFFS, N. J.

Current printing (last number):
10   9   8   7   6   5   4   3   2   1

PRENTICE-HALL INTERNATIONAL, INC. (*London*)
PRENTICE-HALL OF AUSTRALIA, PTY. LTD. (*Sydney*)
PRENTICE-HALL OF CANADA, LTD. (*Toronto*)
PRENTICE-HALL OF INDIA PRIVATE LTD. (*New Delhi*)
PRENTICE-HALL OF JAPAN, INC. (*Tokyo*)

For My Father and Mother

⊷§ PREFACE §⊶

This book is intended to be useful to students coming to *Beowulf* for the first time, and it assumes no knowledge on their part of the Old English language. The background material in the first chapter will seem too much for some and too little or too elementary for others, but I have tried to be guided by my recollection of the questions undergraduates have asked about the poem over the years. (I think, fondly now, of one student who remained gallantly unshaken in his conviction that *Beowulf* was composed in Welsh by Druids, probably at Stonehenge.)

The second and third chapters amount to a critical run-through of the poem, and anyone who would prefer to read them before reading the first chapter will meet no objections in this quarter. A critic working in limited space without the chance to include much textual support for his assertions sometimes feels that he is being alternately pontifical and wishy-washy; any reader enraged by such assertions may be somewhat placated by the solider evidence provided in my recent book, *A Reading of Beowulf* (New Haven, 1968).

I have omitted all but a few footnotes. Those who do any reading in the books mentioned at the end will discover the sources of many of my statements, and I am glad to acknowledge a great general obligation to my predecessors and colleagues in the field of Old English.

The translations of Old English used here are my own and should be tolerated as striving earnestly for plainness and accuracy rather than elegance. That such translations lack one important kind of accuracy—the precision of poetry itself—I will quickly concede. The

ix

use of my own translations also leaves me uncommitted to any one of the various translations of *Beowulf*, about which I do feel obliged, however, to make a few observations here.

Three prose translations readily available in paperbound form can be arranged in order of their degree of literalness. Most literal is that of E. Talbot Donaldson (Norton); somewhat smoother and flatter is that of Constance B. Hieatt (Odyssey); most drastically modified in the direction of prose (*Beowulf* as modern novel) is that of David Wright (Penguin). All share the inability of prose versions to convey much sense of the poetry of the original. On the other hand, a more original and interesting prose translation, that of William Alfred in *Four Medieval Epics* (Modern Library), lacks the smooth readability that ought to be the chief virtue of a prose rendering.

The older verse translation of C. W. Kennedy (Oxford) is still widely used, in part because it employs an alliterative meter in imitation of the original. A more recently published translation, partly in blank verse, is that of Lucien Dean Pearson (Midland). While these versions reproduce certain qualities of the original well, they tend to make the poem seem quainter or cruder than it is and they make no real use of contemporary poetic idiom. Also rather old-fashioned in language is the most recent translation I have seen, that of Kevin Crossley-Holland (Farrar, Straus & Giroux, 1968), a fairly literal version in four-stress lines.

More modern in idiom is the verse translation by Edwin Morgan (California), but its poetic impact is clearly less forceful than that of the translation by Burton Raffel (Mentor). Raffel's translation is a very bold one and suffers from real inaccuracy and distortion in places, but when it is good it is very good. In some respects (the tendency to shift the epic style toward lyric, for instance) it might be compared with Robert Fitzgerald's version of the *Odyssey*.

I must express thanks here to Katherine Gordon-Clark and Andrew Irving for serving expertly as nonexpert readers of portions of the book, and to Maynard Mack for encouragement and some shrewd suggestions for improvements. While there is no way to thank my wife for her part in the writing of this, I could perhaps crave her forgiveness.

⊰§ CONTENTS ੬୬

INTRODUCTION
TO
BEOWULF

❧ I ❧

THE BACKGROUND OF *BEOWULF*

A Prologue with Choice of Scenes
Scene I: The Scop

The king's scop shifts from one foot to the other holding his six-stringed harp close to his ear as he twists a tuning peg. He is hoping to catch the king's eye before the crowd of fighting men in the hall have had too much beer to drink, for he has something much better than the usual blood-and-guts for them this time. Now at last the king sees him and begins to pound loudly on the table with his knife hilt. The roar of talk and laughter dies down, and the scop is waved forward to stand before the packed benches of red-faced warriors. A run of notes and a crash of chords on the harp, and his clear voice begins to chant a tale of the ancient days, speaking the old names in the old phrases of their ancestors. This tale he tells more or less as he learned it from the lips of the old scop at York, but he has since thought of some fine things to add to it—Sigemund's killing of a dragon, for one, and a long death speech for the hero—and he knows from the start that they will like it. . . . At last he finishes singing of the riders circling Beowulf's death mound, and bright tears flash in the eyes of many men in the hall; a moment's pause, and then they cheer and drink his health and hammer on the tables with fists and cups. The king leans forward to toss him down a slender arm ring of pure gold, the finest reward he has ever won for his singing. And now the king's new priest hurries up to bless and embrace him, and to beg him to come after mass next morning and tell it again, slowly, so that the priest can first write it in letters on his wax tablets and then make a great book of it some day, so that men to come

1

will know this tale and it will never pass out of men's memories, just as the old Rome-dwellers, the priest tells him, have left books of their old tales for clerks to read now in the monasteries. The scop sees little point in all this jabber of books, but since he has noted the king's strange liking for this priest he promises to be there in the morning.

Scene II: The Monk

The sputtering goose quill moves more quickly as the grey afternoon light fades in the high library window, the old monk trying to put down a set of verses while they still glow clearly inside his head. To have to write so small slows him down, but the abbot has allotted him only a few precious pieces of parchment for his verses. But it is very wrong to be grudging about it, for the miracle did happen: the abbot did give him leave to write down his "epic" and to read it to the brothers gathered in the dining hall at Yule—at Christmas time. For the abbot has come to understand at long last that it was not only Roman clerks like Virgil who could make long poems full of beautiful meaning out of their old tales but that the English people can do the same with their own tales that everyone loves so well, especially the old monks in this minster. Some say nowadays that it is an evil thing to speak at all of the old heathen times, but surely it cannot be evil to tell of a good man and a good king, and of the courage of men against the cold blackness outside, and of how all things darken and vanish in this transitory world. He has heard of such things in more than one sermon in his time. And because the brothers will listen to his verses they will be moved by the good teaching of his poem, more than they are moved by many a saint's life and homily (though he had not ventured to say that to the abbot). But the best will be some day to recite it in the palace so that the king and his thanes will know in their hearts what is truly noble and royal. The phrases he has heard and spoken so often in his youth when he lived in the world whisper in his ears, float and glow before his eyes. As his pen rushes on he smiles, for he knows he is offering what is best in him now to the glory of God.

FACTS OF HISTORY

We begin our study of the historical context of the Anglo-Saxon poem *Beowulf* with two wholly fictional scenes—suggesting two ways in which the poem may have originated (of which we will have something more to say later)—simply because the scarcity of hard facts drives us toward this kind of speculation. Most of the things a student of literature would like to know about a poem he is reading remain unknown and probably unknowable in the case of *Beowulf*. We know nothing whatever of the identity of the author; we are uncertain of just when and where the poem was composed; we are ignorant of what the Anglo-Saxons themselves may have thought of it, of whether there were any other poems like it at the time, and even of why it came to survive at all. The period of the seventh and eighth centuries in England, the time during which *Beowulf* was probably composed, is neither familiar to the common reader nor very well understood by the historian, for sheer lack of evidence. Men have applied the term "Dark Ages" to this early medieval period primarily in reference to the cultural collapse that followed the fall of the Roman Empire, but the groping historian would be justified in using the term to imply his own ignorance of those times.

We need first to outline a few historical facts about the period. About the year 410 A.D. the last of the Roman legions withdrew from the outlying Roman province of Britain, which had been part of the empire for over 300 years, and the native British were left to face attacks from marauding Picts and Scots from the north and west and from seaborne raiders from the Germanic tribes to the east. Nearly 200 years of intermittent warfare ensued, about which we know very little. A British tradition that seems to go back to this period is the legend of the mighty King Arthur, but we know too little to assume that he was, as some speculate, an actual person, perhaps a certain Artorius, a Romanized Briton who rallied the natives against the invaders. What is clear in its general outlines, however, is the gradual settlement in Britain of various Germanic peoples from what is now Denmark, Germany, and the

Low Countries. These tribes, Angles, Saxons, Jutes, probably also Frisians and Franks, in some instances may have intermarried with the native British population or coexisted beside it, but more often massacred the Britons or drove them back into the hilly western regions of the island. The Angles, the *Engle*, who settled north of the Thames in the two important kingdoms of Northumbria and Mercia, eventually gave their name to the language (*Englisc*) and to the nation as a whole (*Angelcynn* or *Englaland*). We now use the term "Anglo-Saxon" to refer to the people and to the period, but the term "Old English" is more often applied to the language and literature before the Norman Conquest in 1066.

These early Englishmen brought with them from the continent a pagan religion (of which we will have more to say later), but before long they came into close contact with Christianity. The British, who had already been converted to Christianity during the Roman period, had in turn converted the Irish, but they seemed in no hurry to contribute to the salvation of Anglo-Saxon souls. Rome took the first step by sending the missionary Augustine, who arrived in the Kentish capital of Canterbury in the year 597. The subsequent process of conversion continued through most of the seventh century, assisted in the north by Irish missionaries based in such centers as the famous island-monastery of Lindisfarne.

Probably, in some mysterious way, it was the creative clash and fusion of different cultures—Celtic, Roman-Christian, and native Germanic—that led in the north especially to a remarkable cultural flowering known as the Northumbrian Renaissance or the Age of Bede, in reference to the eminent scholar and historian (c. 671–735) of the monastery at Jarrow, whose Latin writings were to become famous all over medieval Europe. Two notable works of art from this period are the beautifully illuminated manuscript of the Lindisfarne Gospels and the Ruthwell Cross, a stone cross eighteen feet high carved with verses from the magnificent devotional poem known as *The Dream of the Rood*. Scholars generally have held the belief for many years that a number of Old English poems, including *Beowulf*, must have formed part of this cultural movement and have been composed at this time.

The original date of composition, it should be understood, is not necessarily the date of the manuscript of *Beowulf*. The only surviving manuscript of the poem, now on display in the British Museum in London, was written about the year 1000. It is known as Cotton Vitellius A. XV, a puzzling label explained by the fact that it once formed part of the collection of Sir Robert Cotton (1571–1631), whose library was catalogued under the names of the various Roman emperors (in this case Vitellius) whose busts adorned his bookcases. Like most surviving Old English manuscripts, this one was probably rescued by a devoted collector from a monastic library at the time of the dissolution of the monasteries decreed by Henry VIII during the English Reformation. By good fortune the *Beowulf* manuscript again survived the threat of a library fire in 1731, though with charred edges. If it had perished then we would have known nothing about it (other than a brief reference by a cataloguer), since the poem was not published in printed form until 1815.

Even though the manuscript must be dated as late as 1000, its language reveals to the expert eye a history of previous copyings, indicating that it was probably composed much earlier. The earliest possible date for the poem would be the year 521 (and by the poem here we must predicate an oral version of it, since the Anglo-Saxons were not able to write it down at that time). In 521 (give or take a few years), we are told by the Frankish historian Gregory of Tours, there was an unsuccessful piratical raid on Frankish territory near the mouth of the Rhine, led by a Scandinavian king whom Gregory calls Chochilaicus. This is beyond doubt the Hygelac who plays a prominent role in *Beowulf* as the hero's liege lord and uncle, and the disastrous raid itself, in which Hygelac was killed, is often mentioned in the poem. Insofar as the events recounted in *Beowulf* are actually historical, they must have taken place at about this time, in the early sixth century.

The date 521 is of course impossibly early. Legend takes a certain length of time to grow and take artistic form; in *Beowulf* historical material like the story of Hygelac seems to have become fused with folk tales of monster fights. More important still, the strong Christian coloring of the poem's language would not have been conceivable before 650 at the very earliest. At the other end of the time scale, the destruction of the northern kingdoms resulting from the Viking raids which began about 800 must put some late limit on the date; some have supposed that a poem celebrating the Danish ancestors of the hated heathen Vikings would hardly have been composed after that date.

We have now narrowed down the range of dates to from 650 to 800, and most scholars seem to place *Beowulf* in the middle of that period, between 700 and 750. Evidence drawn from analysis of the language is not in itself conclusive but tends to support such a relatively early date.

A certain amount of linguistic evidence, furthermore, points to the location of the original version of the poem in Anglian territory, either in Northumbria or Mercia. Although the dialect of the manuscript itself is basically what we call Late West Saxon, the language of the Winchester-based royal court and administrative center, it is heavily larded with words and dialect forms typical of the Anglian regions, the mixed dialect being characteristic of most Old English poetry. There is little else in the poem, however, to indicate where it may have originated. The somewhat abrupt introduction into the poem (lines 1944 ff.) of a laudatory allusion to a continental King Offa who was an ancestral hero of the Mercian royal line (his name was borne by a well-known king of Mercia who ruled from 757 to 796) has led some to argue that the poem was composed for the Mercian court. It might even be significant that another Mercian king in the ninth century was called Wiglaf, the name of the young warrior who succeeds Beowulf at the end of the poem.

But increasingly we have been dealing with speculations. There is not much else in the way of fact that we can bring to the poem. Important questions for the reader of literature remain to be answered, the kinds of questions that, consciously or unconsciously, every reader puts to the works he reads and must answer in some fashion, for better or worse. What kind of mind did the author have? What kind of audience did he address? Under what conditions and in response to what demands did the poem take form? What was the poem for, if it was thought of as having a purpose?

The two imaginary scenes at the head of this chapter may be

useful in helping us gain some provisional answers by the way they attempt to illustrate two current views about the origin of *Beowulf.* Scene I shows the poem being recited at court after it has been "orally" composed by an illiterate minstrel or *scop* (pronounced "shop"); Scene II shows the poem being first composed in writing by a monk.

THE GERMANIC WORLD

The first of these scenes really takes us into the pre-Christian era of Germanic legend and heroic poetry, and into a time before writing was known. (Essentially, writing came to England with the Roman missionaries; the Anglo-Saxons had the runic alphabet earlier but used it only for brief magical or ceremonial inscriptions.) It brings us face to face, therefore, with the much discussed problem of how poetry was composed under such circumstances. Ever since the 1930's when Professor Milman Parry of Harvard collected and recorded a large body of epic verse still being composed and recited by singers in the Balkans, we have had a much clearer understanding of the way such poets re-express and modify their traditional stock of stories. Parry's followers have developed from the evidence what is known as the oral-formulaic theory and have applied it both to the Homeric poems and to *Beowulf,* since the earliest surviving specimens of both Greek and Germanic poetry are obviously closely related to an oral tradition.

The subject is far too complicated and controversial to go into here, but it is worth pointing out that a great many distinctive features of the style of *Beowulf* can only be explained as survivals of an oral tradition. Like Old English poetry generally, *Beowulf* is composed in a special poetic language that contains a great number of often repeated phrases and surprisingly few original phrases. Such repeated phrases are what are usually called formulas. Some epithets applied to King Hrothgar of the Danes will illustrate something of their nature. Apparently there existed in Old English a basic flexible pattern consisting of a word for "king" plus the genitive plural (ending in *-a*) of the name of the people he rules. Thus *Deniga frean* "lord of the Danes" (the word order can be reversed) is three times used of Hrothgar. Since the Danes are often called Scyldings in the poem, four times we find Hrothgar called *frea Scyldinga* "lord of the Scyldings." Many such substitutions can be made within the pattern, such as *wine Scyldinga* "friendly lord of the Scyldings," or *eodor Scyldinga* "protector (literally, fence) of the Scyldings," or *leod Scyldinga* "lord of the Scyldings." Each of these phrases makes a metrical verse. Sometimes an entire line, made up of two verses, may be repeated: three times in the poem we have *Hrothgar mathelode, helm Scyldinga* "Hrothgar spoke, the protector of the Scyldings." In this last instance one can see the usefulness to the poet of the variable formula, for it seems plain that the choice of *helm* was here determined by the need for alliteration on *h*. Once put into circulation by the poets, a formula may appear anywhere in Old English poetry, even in the slightly incongruous contexts of the Christian poetry, where Abraham, for example, becomes *leod Ebrea* "lord of the Hebrews" and Nebuchadnezzar *brego Caldea* "prince of the Chaldeans."

No one would deny that *Beowulf* contains a great many formulas characteristic of the oral tradition, but the real point at issue is whether the poem was composed and given its present form by illiterate poets before it was ever written down. We find a few brief glimpses of how Anglo-Saxon poets may have produced their poetry in the poems themselves. In *Beowulf*, for instance, beginning about line 867, there is an account of the improvising of a new poem by a Danish scop as the warriors ride back to Heorot from their tracking of the wounded Grendel to the haunted mere. Even though this account is not as clear as we would like to have it, we can gather from it that the fictional scop is highly skilled, that he is familiar with many stories of ancient times and that he is able to invent (on horseback) a new poem celebrating Beowulf. He does this by comparing the hero's exploits to those of the famous old hero Sigemund and by sharply contrasting Beowulf's use of his native strength with the disastrous career of the wicked Danish king Heremod.

In another part of the poem, beginning in line 2105, Beowulf describes to his uncle Hygelac the entertainment that was provided for him during his stay in the Danish hall. On this occasion not only the Danish scop but King Hrothgar himself took his turn at reciting verse.

> Then there was song and merriment. The wise old Scylding told of things long ago. Sometimes the brave man brought forth joy from the harp, as he struck the mirthwood. Sometimes he made a poem that was true and painful. Sometimes the greathearted king told a tale of the wonderful. Sometimes again the old warrior, bound by age, chanted a lament for his youth and strength in battle; his heart swelled in him when, heavy with winters, he remembered so much.

Both passages lay stress on the ability to remember the old stories clearly as an important qualification for a poet. The second emphasizes the variety and range of subjects and emotional tones in the repertory.

One might remark incidentally that *Beowulf* itself includes much of the range suggested here. It deals with events in the far past that were believed to be historical or "true"; it contains much that is supernatural or "wonderful"; and its last thousand lines have strong affinities with Hrothgar's lament for the bitter loss of youth and strength.

It is of course possible that these descriptions are not to be taken literally as good evidence of how the poet himself composed. The poem has a certain antiquarian flavor to it, and here the poet might simply be showing us how poets *used to* recite in the old days, just as he shows how funerals used to be before the church put its ban on cremations.

The length of *Beowulf* (3182 lines) also raises questions about the oral origin of the poem. An orally composed poem can be quite long, but the typical oral poem in Germanic literature seems to have been much shorter and less elaborate than *Beowulf*. A fragment of a poem known as *The Fight at Finnsburg* has survived; taking into consideration the speed with which it tells its story, it could hardly have been over 300 lines in its original form. *The Battle of Maldon*, though also incomplete, was probably not much longer. The longer poems in Old English tend to be paraphrases of biblical texts or Latin sermons and must have been the work of a literate poet. Such poems have a style just as "formulaic" as the supposedly freely composed productions of the oral singers. It seems to have been quite possible for a literary poet to imitate the formulaic style. Furthermore, many critics see a kind of artistic polish and structural unity in *Beowulf* that they associate with careful revision of the kind we are familiar with today. Some even believe that the idea of so long and complex a poem must have been suggested in the first place by knowledge of such long Latin poems as the *Aeneid*.

This hasty summary of arguments can do little justice to the complexity of the problem, a problem that will doubtless never be solved to everyone's satisfaction. Perhaps in the end our two scenes need not be mutually exclusive; they may at least form part of the same play. If, on the one hand, some court scop deserves credit for first inventing *Beowulf* in essentially its present form, someone (and someone almost certainly connected with the church) must have written it down and must have modified it in some ways in that very process. If we think of someone writing the poem in the way we think of a poet writing, on the other hand, we must recognize that his debt to the language and patterning of generations of oral singers before him was too great to measure. If we care to indulge our imaginations a little further, we are even free to pretend that our old monk had been in his youth one of those rapt listeners in the king's mead hall, before the time when, like so many of the English in the years after the conversion, he chose to turn his back on the world and enter the monastic life.

In a much more general way, our two scenes may stand for the two cultural worlds that meet in *Beowulf*. The secular world represented by the scop and the king's court is the more important of the two, for out of that Germanic world comes not only the inherited verbal style of the poem, as we have seen, but its basic stories and allusions and meaningful myths, as well as its picture of heroic society and that society's system of values. It is important to recognize that this world is not exclusively Anglo-Saxon, but is a world common to all the Germanic peoples of that period of the great migrations around and through the crumbling Roman Empire.

This period has been called the Heroic Age and has been compared from a sociological point of view with other periods in history that have produced similar literature. Heroic poetry is apparently the product of rather special conditions, often where seminomadic barbarian war bands exist as predators on the fringes of a higher civilization. Such groups carry with them in their raids and journeys what has been called the only entirely portable art, an oral poetry that celebrates a warrior's code perpetually being tested in violent exploits.

Germanic heroic stories are based ultimately, for the most part, on historical events of the fourth, fifth, and sixth centuries, but most of the tales soon acquire the pebble-smooth shape of legend rather than of strict history. These legends transcended national boundaries and circulated freely over an area that, after the migrations, was very large indeed, taking in most of Europe. There is a brief allusion in *Beowulf*, for example, to Eormenric or Ermanaric, a king of the Eastern Goths who ruled an empire that extended from Denmark to the Ukraine before his suicide about the year 375. He became one of the most famous heroes of Germanic legend. The Old English poem *Widsith* (the Far-Traveler) is little more than a storehouse of heroic lore of this kind, usually in the form of a mnemonic list like this one: "Attila ruled the Huns, Eormanric the Goths, Becca the Banings, Gifica the Burgundians, Caesar ruled the Greeks and Cælic the Finns." These sonorous roll calls of heroes and tribes from all over the Germanic world are interspersed with occasional brief anecdotes about individuals.

Since *Beowulf* makes many offhand allusions to such stories, allusions that may have given the original audience special pleasure but merely baffle most modern readers, scholars have had to undertake the patient labor of reconstructing stories, often from scanty information. One of the anecdotal passages in *Widsith* may serve to illustrate the kind of cryptic reference one has to work with.

Hrothulf and Hrothgar, nephew and uncle, kept peace together for the longest time [*or:* a very long time], after they drove into exile the race of Vikings and humbled Ingeld's army, slaughtering the flower of the Heathobard tribe at Heorot. (*Widsith*, lines 45–49)

Now from *Beowulf* we know that Hrothgar had intended to marry his daughter to the Heathobard King Ingeld in an attempt to bring an end to the long-standing feud between the tribes. Beowulf had predicted that the marriage would not work, and the *Widsith* passage confirms his prediction. *Beowulf* also mentions that the hall Heorot was to be burned down in this conflict, but it is not clear just when in the course of the feud this must have happened. Even more cryptic, perhaps, is the way Hrothulf and Hrothgar are mentioned in the quoted passage. From strong hints in *Beowulf* we can gather that young Hrothulf is some day going to usurp the Danish throne from its proper heirs, the sons of his uncle Hrothgar. Such an outcome is probably also suggested in *Widsith* but in a peculiarly ironic way. It is as if one were to remark that from 1775 to 1780 the only two American generals who respected and trusted each other were George Washington and Benedict Arnold. In any event, allusions of this kind compel us to imagine an original audience familiar enough with heroic legend to enjoy recognizing these half-riddling hints. This particular literary pleasure could not have differed much from the response of an alert modern reader to allusive poets like Eliot or Auden.

It is a curious fact that Beowulf himself is never mentioned in the surviving Germanic heroic literature of Scandinavia and the continent. Other characters, especially the members of the Danish dynasty, appear not only in *Widsith* but in later Scandinavian poems and sagas. There Hrothgar appears as Hróarr, though by that time most of the action has shifted to his nephew Hrólfr (the Hrothulf of *Beowulf*) who becomes the hero of his own saga, the Saga of Hrolf Kraki. Scandinavian works also contain references to some of the Geats and Swedes we hear about in the last third of *Beowulf*.

Whether then Beowulf is to be considered a historical character, as these kings and princes seem to have been, has long been the subject of inconclusive debate. No evidence of his existence survives outside the poem but this is not necessarily proof that he was purely fictional. It might as easily be taken to mean that his fame never spread very widely, or that other poems about him have been lost. But those scholars who are skeptical of his historical existence draw attention to certain significant analogues to *Beowulf* taken from a context quite different from the semihistorical context of heroic legend we have been discussing, and that is the context of folklore.

There is a folk tale found in many versions not only in Northern Europe but in other parts of the world that is known as the Bear's Son tale. Here is a summary of its essential features: the hero is usually somehow associated with bears, is descended from bears, or has a name connected with bears; he defends a house against some kind of monstrous enemy; the enemy escapes but is tracked to a hole in the ground; the hero follows him into his lair and kills him, the hero's companions meanwhile losing heart and deserting him; something valuable is brought back by the hero as a trophy of his success. The resemblances of this story to *Beowulf* are undeniable. In the first place, one good guess at the meaning of the name Beowulf is that it means "bee-wolf," that is, an enemy to bees, a honey-eater, a bear. Beowulf's peculiarly bear-like habit of hugging his enemies to death is described in the poem. In the poem's action, Beowulf defends Heorot against the monster Grendel, who escapes to his underwater home after losing his arm in the fight; Beowulf later invades that home in search of Grendel's mother, who has attacked the hall to gain vengeance for her son, and kills the female monster, while up above the waiting Danes lose hope and go back to their hall; the hero brings back as trophies Grendel's head and the great hilt of a giant sword.

Even these clear connections with folk tale do not, however, resolve the problem of historical truth, for stories of this fabulous sort can easily be attached to quite historical figures. There was, after all, a Col. David Crockett. The version of the Bear's Son tale closest to *Beowulf* in most details is found in the thirteenth-century Icelandic *Grettis Saga,* which is based on the actual life of the famous outlaw Grettir, who died in Iceland in the year 1031. At one time scholars generally regarded Beowulf as a folktale character inserted arbitrarily into a context of semihistorical legend. It has recently been suggested that history and fable cannot be so easily separated, since battles with underworld creatures are elsewhere associated with members of ruling Scandinavian families, especially the Gautar or Geats to which Beowulf is said to belong.[1] Perhaps some ancient royal ritual is reflected in these stories. The possibility that some historical model for the character of Beowulf really existed has not been entirely ruled out.

Comparison of the plot of *Beowulf* with the plots of folk tales can be seriously misleading, however, if it is meant to imply that the poem is at bottom childish or trivial. Indeed more than one scholar and critic has voiced a certain contempt for the poem on these grounds. But there is certainly no reason why a folktale plot may not form the basis of an action that is charged with moving and complex significance. The main plot of *King Lear* is nothing but a fairy tale of an old man and his three daughters.

When an action attains a certain degree of significance, it is likely to be called a myth, and the term myth has often been applied to *Beowulf*, though, to be sure, not always with the same meaning in each case. The scientific-minded anthropologists of the nineteenth century were, for example, given to equating Beowulf with the life-giving forces of the sun and Grendel with diseases associated with marshy ground. Some recent allegorists have tried to explain the poem by using the Christian myth, and thereby representing Beowulf as unregenerate Everyman and the dragon and Grendel as mere manifestations of Satan. More interesting and subtle parallels have been suggested by such historians of early religions as Mircea Eliade, who have furnished abundant evidence of primitive myths of creation and of the cosmic battle between chaotic and divine forces that seem very close to some of the symbolic patterns in *Beowulf*.

Obviously one important element to consider in studying the mythic background of the poem is the nature of the pre-Christian Englishman's way of viewing the world. Here we have very little information to build on, since it was not in the church's interest to perpetuate heathen beliefs by committing them to writing. Most of our knowledge of Germanic mythology comes from the much later and rather sophisticated Eddic literature of Iceland. Here we find tales of Thor's battles with the frost giants; descriptions of Asgard, the city of the gods where one-eyed Odin rules, and of Valhalla, the hall of the slain-in-battle to which Valkyries bring the heroic dead; and the memorable account of the twilight of the gods, the last battle in which gods and heroes go down fighting together against the demonic forces of destruction, against giant wolf and world-encircling serpent. We have no way of knowing how much the heathen Anglo-Saxons knew of these stories, but the tales do reflect a general world view that could hardly have been unfamiliar to them, a picture of a universe encompassed by hostile darkness, sustained only by the heroic efforts of men and gods, doomed to ultimate extinction.

In a famous passage from Bede's *Ecclesiastical History of the English People,* one of the advisers of King Edwin of Northumbria, during the course of a debate in the year 627, describes a world much like this:

> Thus, O king, the present life of men on earth, in comparison with that time which is unknown to us, appears to me to be as if, when you are sitting at supper with your ealdormen and thegns in the winter-time, and a fire is lighted in the midst and the hall warmed, but everywhere outside the storms of wintry rain and snow are raging, a sparrow should come and fly rapidly through the hall, coming in at one door, and immediately out at the other. Whilst it is inside, it is not touched by the storm of winter, but yet, that tiny space of time gone in a moment, from winter at once returning to winter, it is lost to your sight. Thus this life of men appears for a little while; but of what is to follow, or of what went before, we are entirely ignorant.[2]

Bede's parable of the pagan view of life has a certain similarity to the metaphysical world of *Beowulf.* A central image in the poem is the warm and lighted hall set in contrast with the menacing darkness outside. At the beginning of the poem, the community in the Danish hall is threatened by Grendel, who comes in darkness; Beowulf succeeds in expanding the circle of light first by driving Grendel away and later by exorcizing the evil mere where the monsters live; when he becomes king of his own country, he holds off the enemies until his own death in battle against the dragon, at which time darkness seems to close swiftly in on the kingdom Beowulf will no longer be able to guard. While a few scattered phrases in *Beowulf* can be taken as referring to a life after death (for example, after his death Beowulf is said to pass "into God's protection"), the overwhelming impression the poem gives is of the irreversible movement of men and their civilizations into the blackness of oblivion. This dark background sets off the naked and absolute quality of Germanic heroism, a courage-in-spite-of that asserts itself in a world without hope.

THE CHRISTIAN WORLD

Despite the poem's many links with an older Germanic period, however, it originated within a Christian context and, at least in its present form, shows strong traces of this influence, traces which seem to form part of its very structure rather than being superficial or casual additions. Our second imaginary scene, showing the poet-monk at work in the monastic library, is intended to suggest the immediate background of *Beowulf* in eighth-century England. It offers a tentative explanation for a most important question to which we have not yet found a really satisfactory answer: if *Beowulf* was essentially a heathen poem, how was it able to survive at a time when all recording and preservation of literature lay wholly in the hands of churchmen?

In the scene, our fictional monk prefers to believe that the poem's values are not in fact incompatible with those of Christianity, although he may feel a few obscure twinges of conscience about this assumption from time to time. He is even ready to include the poem among the edifying mealtime readings to the brothers which St. Benedict prescribed in his monastic rule, but he is aware that not every abbot is as liberal as his. In 797 Alcuin of York, a well-known English scholar who became chief educational adviser to Charlemagne, wrote back to the bishop of Lindisfarne: "Let the words of God be read at the priests' mealtimes. It is proper then to hear a reader, not a harp player, to listen to the discourses of the fathers, not the poems of the heathen. For what has Ingeld to do with Christ? The house is narrow; it cannot contain them both." [3] Alcuin's remarks, which echo many earlier condemnations of secular literature by the fathers of the church, show a point of view decidedly hostile to the recitation or preservation by clerks of poems like *Beowulf*; on the other hand, they also betray the fact that educated ecclesiastics in 797 still took a lively interest in such stories as that of Ingeld of the Heathobards, a minor figure in *Beowulf*.

One would very much like to know what the Anglo-Saxons themselves thought about *Beowulf*. One would expect that a poem of such excellence would be frequently mentioned, but the incredible fact is that we have no absolute proof that anyone, outside of a few copyists, ever read or heard this poem until the early nineteenth century when it was first published. Probably no one during the later Middle Ages and early Renaissance was able to make much sense out of Old English poetry, although a few could read the prose. Many scholars believe that one Old English poem known as *Andreas*, an account of the missionary career of St. Andrew, shows some direct imitation of *Beowulf*, but a relationship like this is not easy to demonstrate, given the conventional and formulaic nature of Old English poetic diction. Otherwise there is silence.

It may be that a little information as to how the poem was regarded can be drawn from the manuscript in which it appears. It is there combined with *Judith*, a biblical poem describing the Hebrew heroine's beheading of Holofernes, and with several prose accounts of fabulous marvels in India and the East. Is it possible that whoever put the manuscript collection together about the year 1000 included *Beowulf* because it contained interesting descriptions of monsters and dragons? We can only add this to our long list of open questions.

A good deal of Old English poetry besides *Beowulf* has survived, though probably only a small fraction of what once existed, and much of it was probably composed during the same general period. From it we can learn something in a general way about the literary context of the times. Most of the surviving poetry is religious. Bede tells a famous story about the Yorkshire cowherd Cædmon, a lay brother in the monastery at Whitby, who had to slip away in mortification from the gatherings where the harp was passed from hand to hand and men took their turns in reciting poems, until the moment when he was divinely inspired to produce poetry in the old measures on Christian subjects. This story, which may be understood as something like a myth of origin for the Christian poetry, has led scholars to use the term Cædmonian to describe early religious verse of a narrative kind, such as the retelling of the biblical story of the Exodus from Egypt, in which Moses is represented as a loyal retainer of God the King and as the indomitable chieftain of the Israelites. Some of this Cædmonian verse was probably composed even earlier than *Beowulf*. It has been pointed out that the Christian references that occur in *Beowulf* seem to follow in an already established tradition of religious formulas. It may well be that a poem like *Beowulf* could appear only after a period of familiarization not only with such formulas but with the idea of long narrative poems, and only after the newly converted English were secure enough in their faith to take up a story of the old heathen times.

The religious poems are often of considerable length: the composite poem *Genesis* is almost as long as *Beowulf*. Whether nonreligious poems on this scale other than *Beowulf* ever existed is not known. We do have a fragment, containing some sixty lines, of an Old English poem know as *Waldere* which was accidentally discovered in the Royal Library in Copenhagen in 1860. Since we happen to know this story from other sources, we can surmise from the leisurely pace of the narrative that *Waldere* must have been a poem of some length, probably at least a thousand lines long, and conceivably as long as *Beowulf*. The existence of *Waldere* does lead one to suspect that we may have lost some other long secular poems that have perished without trace, but such a suspicion cannot be proved.

A different kind of relationship exists between certain passages in *Beowulf* and a group of shorter poems known as the elegies, including such well-known works as *The Wanderer, The Seafarer,* and *The Ruin*. The relationship lies in similarities of style and tone. That so many attempts have been made to categorize the elegies as either fundamentally "Christian" or "secular" demonstrates very clearly how hard it is to break down the strange fusion of traditions so characteristic of Old English poetry, and indeed of Anglo-Saxon culture generally. Although on the one hand the elegies reflect the medieval laments over mortality and mutability that one can readily find in Latin sermons of the time, they are also closely related to the older heroic world. The speakers in the elegies (and in the elegiac passages in *Beowulf* which will be discussed later) typically confront ruins: the ruins of a crumbling Roman city, of a once secure feudal relationship to a now dead lord, of a love affair broken off abruptly by feud or exile. In each instance action, which is always the solution in heroic poetry, is made impossible; the speakers can only give eloquent expression to their suffering. Perhaps their passivity is in itself an emblem of a heroic world now felt to be on the point of vanishing away. The same kind of sad retrospection dominates the latter part of *Beowulf* and may itself be an important "Christian element," somewhat paradoxically. For only his firm footing in Christianity can give the poet the self-confidence to look back for what is recoverable from the great pagan past and perhaps even to mourn its passing.

Although its author was almost certainly a Christian, *Beowulf* is not a Christian poem in the sense that its value system is otherworldly or even that it reflects specifically Christian ethical principles. With remarkable consistency the poet succeeds in representing his characters as sober monotheists who frequently invoke the Deity, but there are no references in the poem to Christ, the saints, or the church. In this way he can present Hrothgar and Beowulf as noble pagans who talk very much like Christians without really being Christians. In only one place in the poem are the Danes called heathens (lines 175–88), and this passage is so much at odds with everything else in the poem that some have taken it to be a later addition by someone other than the author. In this passage the Danes, under the pressure of Grendel's merciless attacks, are said to revert to the worship of heathen gods and are sharply condemned for it.

The Christian references in the poem are relatively few in number and seem indeed to have been carefully chosen to fit smoothly into an already established secular context. We can see this in several examples. After the great surge of creative power that results in the building of the mead hall Heorot, Hrothgar's scop appropriately sings his first song in it, not some Germanic lay, but a hymn about God's creation of the universe as it is described in Genesis. In another instance, Grendel's evil attributes as a humanoid destroyer who preys on society are expanded rather than essentially changed by the poet's addition of the story of Grendel's descent from Cain. Cain, the first fratricide and disrupter of human order, fits perfectly into the pre-existing Germanic role of outlaw and exile. Hrothgar's long speech to Beowulf (beginning in line 1700) has enough Christian tone and imagery to be customarily known as Hrothgar's sermon, but its moral lesson—that a man must recognize that he cannot live forever in prosperity—is not exclusively Christian. It is likely that a few softening touches of gentleness and altruism have been added to the hero's character, but Beowulf still remains basically the ideal Germanic warrior rather than the Christ figure that some have claimed to see in him.

THE SOCIETY OF THE POEM

At first the modern reader may find the society pictured in *Beowulf* strange and even unattractive. It may strike him as barbaric—almost American—in its obsession with violence and its unrepentant passion for showy material things, and yet at the same time sophisticated in its sure awareness of the depth and complexity of certain human values and relationships. But the twentieth-century mind, overwhelmed by our world's intricate relativities, will above all find this society to be simple and limited in scope.

Obviously it is historical fact that eighth-century society was far simpler than ours, but the fictional society represented in *Beowulf* (and in heroic poetry generally) is even simpler than the reality of those times. The poetry is the product of a single aristocratic class of warriors and it is directed exclusively to the interests of such an audience. This means that the reader certainly cannot approach the poem as if it were a realistic novel, for large areas of reality are deliberately excluded from the poem. The characters feast constantly, but we never see peasants engaged in growing their food or brewing their ale. The warriors' weapons are all inherited from the old days, and we never see them being forged by real smiths. The warriors are never seen at work. If they are not fighting they are drinking, boasting or listening to a scop's replay of some of the fights of old. Their world is as severely restricted as the world of Jane Austen's novels. In this respect, the characters in *Beowulf* are more like the warriors of the *Iliad* than the civilian hero Odysseus, who shows his skill at many different accomplishments besides fighting.

The opening lines of the poem may serve as a brief epitome of the central values of this warrior class.

> Hear me—we have heard tell of the strength of Spear-Danes, great kings, in days long past, and of how those princes carried courage into action! (1–3)

The poet announces at the outset that his theme is to be strength and courage, and the kind of strength and courage that survives oblivion by being remembered by men through the poet's words. Fame is indeed the spur: to live and die bravely and publicly is all, for then something of a man will live on in the thoughts of other warriors. And *we,* audience and poet together, become at once important, because we remember the names and guarantee the glory, as we hope other men will some day do for us.

Personal and individual as it is, this drive toward fame is also the structural basis of heroic society. The social order is created by an individual's energy, as we can see in the story of the fabled Scyld that serves as prologue to the poem. The poet describes his coming to rescue the lordless Danes from anarchy and to establish the Scylding dynasty in which his name will live for all time. A destitute child when he arrives mysteriously in a boat from somewhere across the sea, Scyld expands his power through aggressive action against the neighboring tribes until he obtains their submission and tribute. That was a good king, the poet exclaims, that is the way for a king to act. But what has been won by force must now be maintained by other means. Through the God-sanctioned birth of a son to Scyld a dynasty is established, but this alone will not insure a secure future for the Danes unless the young prince realizes that he must win his subjects' loyalty and affection by generous gifts. Generosity is the second great obligation of a king, as the poet points out in a typically sententious way.

In the ensuing description of Scyld's funeral, we see more than mere prowess and prudence, however; we see the moving intensity of the bond of love that exists ideally between a great king and his loyal people. Scyld's body is placed in a treasure-laden ship, which is then sent drifting out to sea toward some unknowable destination. If we are to understand the values of the poem fully, we must realize that the great treasures that his people bring him in death—ancient weapons and coats of mail, a golden standard— are wholly symbolic representations of their grief and love, and that these objects travel outward with their king almost like retainers in a somber procession. Even though, like Bede's sparrow, Scyld must now leave the lighted hall, he travels perpetually wreathed in the grateful memory of his people.

The warriors we have been speaking of so far belong to that inner group of picked men known as the comitatus, a Latin word meaning retinue that has been borrowed from the first full description of the Germanic people by the Roman historian Tacitus in his *Germania,* written in 98 A.D. Some of the native terms used for this group in *Beowulf* may suggest something of the nature of their relationship to each other and to their king or lord: friends, kinsmen, table comrades, hearth comrades, hall-sitters, hand companions (i.e., close at hand). By the conventions of heroic poetry, and often enough in the actual practice of Anglo-Saxon society, these aristocrats were bound by a sacred oath of homage to defend their lord and to avenge his death at all costs. The famous entry under the year 755 in *The Anglo-Saxon Chronicle* tells of a king surprised by a group of enemies and how the members of his comitatus bore themselves:

And then the king . . . went to the door and then gallantly defended himself until he caught sight of the prince, and then rushed out on him and severely wounded him; and they all set on the king until they had slain him. And then from the woman's cries the king's thanes became aware of the disturbance, and whoever was then ready and quickest ran thither; and the prince offered each of them money and life, and none of them would accept it, but they went on fighting continuously until they all lay slain, except one Welsh hostage, and he was badly wounded.[4]

Some of the members of the comitatus were actually closely related to the king by blood, but tradition usually went further in regarding the entire tribe or clan as symbolically sharing in the intimate bond of a single family. The ideal of such a tightly knit human community and the absolute obligations of loyalty it imposed persisted throughout the Anglo-Saxon period, as we can see very clearly in the intensely heroic tone of the eleventh-century poem on the Battle of Maldon, and indeed much of the same ideal lived on in the feudal and chivalric codes of the later Middle Ages. Christianity undoubtedly tried to temper the savagery of the ideal, but even the noted Christian teacher and administrator Aldhelm, in a letter written about the year 700 to the clergy of an exiled bishop, exhorting them to remain faithful to their leader, used an analogy from secular life as his strongest argument:

> Behold, if laymen, ignorant of the divine knowledge, abandon the faithful lord whom they have loved during his prosperity, when his good fortune has come to an end and adversity befallen him, and prefer the safe ease of their sweet native land to the afflictions of their exiled lord, are they not regarded by all as deserving of ridicule and hateful jeering, and of the clamour of execration? What then will be said of you if you should let the pontiff who has fostered you and raised you go into exile alone?[5]

It will be evident, however, that powerful centrifugal and disruptive forces must always have been felt in a society so dedicated to aggressive behavior and the strutting niceties of personal honor. Murder and anarchy are common in early English society and in the events recounted in *Beowulf*. Since law in our sense scarcely existed, private vengeance usually had the task of dealing with such crises. As we see often in *Beowulf*, such private vengeance had a way of leading to a long-lasting and bloody feud or vendetta. The vendetta was such an unsatisfactory solution to the problem of violence that an alternative system which substituted the payment of fines for taking the lives of enemies already existed in early times and was later elaborately developed in the laws of the Anglo-Saxon kings. This is the system of the wergild, which sets a fixed monetary value not only on the life of each man in each rank of society—a nobleman's life was worth a good deal more than a peasant's—but also on any part of a man's person that might suffer injury. We are told in the poem, for instance, that Beowulf's own father Ecgtheow, having killed a man, had been compelled to flee into exile in Denmark, presumably to escape from vengeful relatives; there King Hrothgar had settled the feud by sending "ancient treasures" to the victim's kinsmen.

Another device often resorted to in an attempt to bring the long-term enmity between feuding tribes to a stop was the political marriage. In *Beowulf,* as was mentioned earlier, Hrothgar plans to marry his daughter to the son of his ancient enemy, King Froda of the Heathobards, in order to insure peace, and the Danish princess Hildeburh in the Finn episode was married to King Finn of the Frisians probably with the same end in view. The device is rarely successful, as Beowulf himself pithily remarks: "But it is usually very rare that the killing spear lies still for even a short space of time after the fall of a prince, no matter how fine the bride may be!" (lines 2029–31). And when the smoldering fires of conflict break out again, the women in *Beowulf* must assume the painful role of helpless victims rather than "peace-weavers," often now having kinsmen on both sides. The Old English poem *Genesis* gives us a vivid cameo picture of a woman enslaved after military defeat:

> Many a bright-cheeked girl had to go frightened and trembling into a stranger's embrace, for the guardians of women and treasure had fallen dead from wounds.

In most societies, up until relatively modern times, a man found meaning primarily in his existence as a significant part of society, in the well-defined role that he accepted and played. That an individual might wish to take a stance opposed to society in order to actualize his own unique potential is an idea which most members of such tradition-directed societies could scarcely have comprehended, even though the idea is certainly implicit in Christianity. For the Germanic heroic world, a man outside society can only be the pitiable or contemptible figure of exile or outlaw, driven by great necessity out into the darkness away from mankind and represented as suffering agony in his longing to return and become "real" again. The Old English elegies already mentioned, particularly *The Wanderer*, give poignant expression to this kind of suffering. As we will see shortly, in *Beowulf* it is the monster Grendel who plays to some extent this traditional role of outcast and exile.

If we have laid stress here on the importance of the social role, the reader may with some justification make the objection that epic poetry is based on the concept of a hero, and that a hero is by very definition an intense individualist. Can we even conceive of heroism without individuality? Obviously not, but epic heroes may differ in the degree to which they act in consonance with the aims of their own society, even though they are not in actual opposition to those aims, as tragic heroes often are. In the *Iliad*, Achilles must force the other Achaeans to admit his unique greatness before he will consent to function again as a part of the Greek host, and even then he comes into battle because his close friend Patroclus has been killed. Beowulf, on the other hand, never comes into such conflict with his society, largely because almost all his heroic energies are consistently directed outward toward nonhuman antagonists. That he is different from other men and surpasses them is assuredly made clear in the poem but by devices other than those used by Homer, as we will see in the next chapter.

ARTIFACTS AND CUSTOMS

Archeology can help give us some picture of the physical world of the poem, if we make the reasonable assumption that the poet, like most medieval artists, was describing a world much like the world his audience was familiar with. Our appreciation of the material richness of early Anglo-Saxon culture has been greatly enhanced by the extraordinary archeological discovery at Sutton Hoo in Eastern England in 1939. There a large oval mound or barrow above a riverbank was excavated, revealing the outline of a large ship that had been buried in it. This clearly was a royal ship-burial of the pre-Christian kind, even though coins found in the

treasure that had been placed in the burial ship date the burial between 650 and 660, a time when East Anglia had supposedly been
converted to Christianity. Probably the most impressive objects
found at Sutton Hoo are the superb pieces of jewelry, mostly of gold
with garnet insets, now on display in the British Museum. But other
items in the find are of interest to readers of *Beowulf*. There are
gold-adorned weapons and a mask-helmet like those Hrothgar gives
Beowulf; there is a royal standard like the one placed on Scyld's funeral ship; and there are the fragments of a small harp, the first ever
discovered. Enough of the harp remained to allow replicas to be
constructed and actually played. The inclusion in the hoard of a
pair of silver spoons with an apparently Christian inscription indicates that we may see in this burial the same curious blending of
Christian and pagan that *Beowulf* shows in its own way.

Art historians have pointed to the close resemblance between
some of the Sutton Hoo artifacts and Swedish artifacts of the same
period. This has led some to wonder whether *Beowulf* itself, with
its Swedish setting, might not have originated at this East Anglian
royal court, and (to go further into tempting speculation) whether
the ancestors of this East Anglian dynasty, known as the Wuffings,
may not have been refugees from Beowulf's own Geatish kingdom
in Southern Sweden.[6]

A safer conclusion we can draw from Sutton Hoo is that the descriptions in *Beowulf* of priceless treasures, royal munificence and
aristocratic elegance are not merely (as they were once thought to
be) the starved fancies of some nostalgic poet but recognizable if
somewhat idealized reflections of contemporary court life. Furthermore, the artistic excellence of the Sutton Hoo finds makes less sur-
prising the excellence of the poem, for we can have little doubt that
we are dealing with a high level of culture.

The close relationship of Sutton Hoo to the poem is startlingly
illustrated by the fact that passages from *Beowulf* were actually introduced as evidence in 1939 in the coroner's inquest to determine
the ownership and legal status of the treasure. The legal issue was
whether or not the original buriers of the treasure had had the in-
tention of coming back to recover it. Such passages from the poem
as the Last Survivor's speech (2246 ff.) helped establish to the jury's

satisfaction that the Anglo-Saxons must have been committing it to the earth permanently.

Another recent discovery casts some light on the royal palaces described in the poem. The ground plan of the buildings in the royal township of Old Yeavering, near the present border between England and Scotland, where King Edwin of Northumbria ruled in the seventh century, has been revealed, first by aerial photography and then by careful excavation, even though the wooden structures themselves have vanished entirely. Among the discoveries were the foundations of an immense hall, the traces of a large wooden grandstand in the shape of a Roman theater, presumably for outdoor assemblies, and a building which is believed to be a heathen temple converted to use as a Christian church.

We may conjecture that Hrothgar's domain at Heorot may have looked something like a frontier fort in pioneer America, with a number of wooden buildings of various sizes enclosed by an earthwork or a palisade wall. The protective wall or stockade was called a *tun* by the Anglo-Saxons, the original of our word "town." It was probably from such an outer wall that the frightened Danes listened to the screams of Grendel in his battle with Beowulf inside Heorot.

The great hall itself was a lofty barnlike structure, built of heavy timber held together with iron reinforcing bands. The gold-plated roof that covers Heorot is symbolically sound but architecturally unlikely. In the usual Germanic hall, fires burned along a central hearth running down the middle of the building, and on the two floored sides of the hall benches and trestle tables were placed by day, while a high seat was provided for the king. By night the warriors slept on the floor or on the benches, their weapons hung along the walls. The king and queen slept not in the hall but in a smaller separate building called the *bur* (our word "bower"). Beowulf is also sleeping in a *bur* when Grendel's mother attacks on the second night.

Since Heorot is constantly referred to as a beer hall, mead hall or wine hall, festive drinking by the king and his comitatus was obviously one of its principal activities. Queen Wealhtheow and her daughter walk through the great hall serving out ceremonial drinks from precious cups to host and guests in a ritual order of precedence. Entertainment by a scop was furnished at the feast: Hrothgar's scop sings the story of creation and the tale of Finn and Hengest, and King Hrothgar himself performs, we are told later. Another important kind of ritual in the hall was the exchange of gifts. Beowulf formally presents his trophies to Hrothgar after he returns from the mere, and the king then gives spectacular presents to Beowulf and his men in reward for their valor. In heroic poetry at least, a principal form of currency was the gold arm ring, which had the advantages of being valuable, portable, and showy; hence the king is always being referred to as "ring giver."

Little need be said of the ships in the poem, since they are much like the popular idea of the Viking ship—large open rowing boats with a single mast and square sail, and high prows and sterns. The ship buried in the mound at Sutton Hoo was over eighty feet long; it was not, however, fitted with mast and sail. Poets call the ships "ring-prowed," perhaps in reference to the curving or curling-over of the extremity of the prow.

Weapons and armor play a great part in the poem, on the symbolic as well as the merely decorative level. The fully equipped warrior in *Beowulf* wears a flexible mail shirt, a byrnie, made of small interlocking iron rings. The poet calls it "ring net," "breast net," or "battle garment" and often draws attention to the skill and patient handlabor required in its manufacture. (In real life a byrnie was probably far too expensive an item for most men.) On his head the warrior wears a helmet, perhaps like the one unearthed at Sutton Hoo, which was made of iron and bronze with a masklike front complete with finely wrought metal eyebrows, nose and mustache and furnished with eyeholes to see through. On his helmet may be the figures of boars, originally magical symbols of pagan origin, probably once associated with the Germanic fertility god Freyr.

His principal weapon is the sword, often with its own name. Beowulf's sword is called Nægling, or "the son of nail(s)," either in reference to some studded decorations on it or simply to its manufacture from iron nails. That iron was once thought to be quite rare and valuable is evident from the apparently unnecessary formula "the edge was iron" that is often applied to swords, a formula that may go back to the Bronze Age. The older the sword, the better its quality; family heirlooms with a long history were favored by heroes and poets. The elaborately decorated hilt of the sword often had an ornamental ring attached to it (hence probably the term "ring sword"), and perhaps also a runic inscription to add magic powers. The blade is referred to as being wavy or woven together, perhaps alluding to a process of welding or decoration that left wavy patterns in the metal of the blade.

The warrior carries a spear for throwing, with a shaft made of ash and an iron tip, and protects himself with a round shield made of linden wood, with a metal rim and a knob or boss in the center. The iron shield that Beowulf had made to protect himself from the dragon's fire would have been considered extraordinary. The warrior may also carry a *seax* (the weapon from which the Saxons probably derived their name), a long dagger like the one with which Grendel's mother attacks Beowulf during the fight in the underwater cave. Bows and arrows are mentioned in the poem, but it seems likely that, as sometimes in the *Iliad* where archery is associated with the rather cowardly Paris, the bow was not regarded as a particularly heroic weapon.

THE INHERITED STYLE

Beowulf was composed in an alliterative stress verse that was the common property of all early Germanic peoples but which differs from most modern English verse almost as much as the language of the poem differs from ours in other respects. Both meter and language can be illustrated in the following passage from the original, here followed by a translation that tries to mimic some of the sound effects of the Old English.

> Fyrst forth gewat;   flota wæs on ythum,
> bat under beorge.   Beornas gearwe
> on stefn stigon,   —streamas wundon,
> sund with sande;   secgas bæron
> on bearm nacan   beorhte frætwe,
> guthsearo geatolic;   guman ut scufon,
> weras on wilsith   wudu bundenne.[7] (210–16)

> Fast fared the time;   floater was in ocean,
> boat under bankside.   Bowmen lightly
> on stern stepping   —streams were mingling,
> sea with sand then—   swiftly carried
> to boat-storage   brightest treasures,
> glittering war gear;   gallants out shoved then,
> warriors on willed trip   wood-braced vessel.

Seven lines of a translation this peculiar put considerable strain on the reader, but they serve the purpose of showing how difficult it is to imitate closely the rhythm of the original and still make tolerable sense in modern English. As everyone knows, it is generally almost impossible to transfer poetic meaning, with its subtle but strong textures of sound and sense, from one language into another. From one point of view, of course, Old English is not entirely another language: the reader unfamiliar with it may still be able to recognize such words here as *forth, wæs, streamas, sande,* or *wudu.* But rhythmically it is a different language. During the course of the development of Old English into modern English, inflectional endings on words were generally lost at the same time that prepositions and definite articles became much more common, and this change makes all the difference in the world to the basic rhythms of both speech and poetry. In our passage, for instance, the verse *sund with sande* (literally "sea against sand") has a falling or trochaic rhythm ($\stackrel{\angle}{} \times \stackrel{\angle}{} \times$) because the dative form of *sand* in Old English is *sande* and the word for "the" can be dispensed with in poetry. On the other hand, the equivalent for this in modern English would be *the sea against the sand* ($\times \stackrel{\angle}{} \times \stackrel{\angle}{} \times \stackrel{\angle}{}$), a phrase that would fall naturally into the iambic pattern that has dominated English poetry since Chaucer's time and that would in fact fit the iambic trimeter line of ballad meter.

In the quoted passage, the reader can ascertain for himself the underlying trochaic pattern of this verse, with its heavy initial stresses, usually further emphasized by alliteration or initial rhyme, as in *bat/beorge/beornas,* or *stefn/stigon/streamas.* This kind of verse counts its stresses rather than the total number of syllables in a line or half line: *súnd with sánde* has 4 syllables, *bát under béorge* ("boat under hill") has 5, and a verse like *hábbath we to thæm mǽran* (a few lines further on—"we have [business] with the famous one") has as many as 7, but this does not matter so long as each verse has only two main stresses. The two verses of each line are linked by alliteration: the first verse may have either one or two alliterating stresses, the second verse only one.

Problems arise with many verses that seem to begin with unstressed syllables and thus to have a different rhythm altogether: an example would be the verse, *under Héorotes hróf* ("under Heorot's roof"), with this pattern of stresses: x x x́ x x ⌣́. Professor John C. Pope of Yale has proposed the attractive hypothesis that originally the harp may have been used to sound a note or chord at the beginning of such verses, thus replacing the stress that would ordinarily have fallen on a spoken or chanted word. We cannot, however, be certain just how the poet used the harp, although we are often told that it was used to accompany the reciting of poetry.

In the same quoted passage we can find examples of the practice of variation, a notable feature of Germanic poetry, where the poet will use several words or phrases in quick succession to refer to the same object or action. In the first sentence the boat is called *flota* ("floater") and *bat* ("boat"). Later the men who embark on it are called *beornas, secgas, guman,* and *weras,* all words meaning "men," and perhaps originally showing fine distinctions in meaning that we find it hard to recover now. Of these four words only *weras* would also be used in prose or in ordinary speech; the others would have been instantly recognized by Anglo-Saxons as words that poets use, just as we can identify in old-fashioned verse such words as *o'er, ope, yore, hath, 'twas* as "poetic."

From a practical point of view, Anglo-Saxon poets also needed a large stock of such interchangeable synonyms or near-synonyms in order to meet the unrelenting demands of alliteration in each line. Like anything else, variation can become tiresome when it is used badly (as it often is in Old English poetry), but in the hands of a skilled poet like the poet of *Beowulf* it is sometimes used to sketch out, with that kind of economy and directness especially character-istic of poetry, the various aspects of a character or situation. In the Grendel-fight, for example, the way the Danes first hear only a strange "sound" issuing from the hall and then come to identify it

and recognize its implications is dramatized by successive variations (here italicized):

> *Sound* mounted up, again and again; hideous fear came upon the
> North-Danes, upon each of them who heard that *lament,* heard God's
> enemy sing a *lay of terror,* a *song without victory,* heard hell's prisoner
> bewail his pain. (782b–788a)

An important feature of the vocabulary of Old English poetry was
the poetic compound, a traditional form of concentrated metaphor.
The most striking form of compound to us is the kenning (a term
borrowed for convenience from Old Norse). The following are examples of kennings: *hronrad,* "whale riding place," or *ganotes bæth,*
"seabird's bath," for the sea; *beadoleoma,* "battle light," or *hamera
laf,* "what the (smith's) hammers leave," or *guthwine,* "war friend,"
for a sword; *woruldcandel,* "world candle," for the sun, and *mere-
hrægl,* "sea garment," for a ship's sail. Such compounds and phrases
formed part of the inherited poetic language of Anglo-Saxon poets.
No doubt individual poets invented new ones from time to time, but
most of these expressions were as stereotyped as Homer's rosy-fingered
dawn. The *Beowulf* poet differs from other poets of the time only in
the relatively large number of compounds he uses and the imagina-
tive way in which he uses them. One might well expect so conventional a style to lack freshness and vitality, but for some reason it
does not. The very compression of the kennings and of phrases like
them succeeds in charging the verse with a consistently high level of
metaphorical energy. Perhaps one might even say that the mosaic
of the larger poem is built up out of many tiny "poems" in the form
of these expressions, giving the surface a texture of interesting depth.

Another steady source of poetic power is the alliteration itself,
which often effectively underlines a rhetorical point or a thematic
contrast. A simple example can be found in the following verses describing Grendel after he has driven the Danes out of their hall and
moved in:

> Heorot eardode,
> sincfage sel sweartum nihtum. (166–67)

He lived in Heorot, in that treasure-bright (*sincfage*) hall in the black
(*sweartum*) nights.

Sincfage sel calls to our minds not only the dazzling physical appearance of the gold-roofed hall but also the vital functioning of the heroic community within it, as this functioning is typically symbolized by the giving and receiving of treasure. All this then is here set aaginst *sweartum nihtum,* with its suggestion of the annihilating blackness of Grendel's world of destruction and death.

In its small way this example is typical of the use of strong contrast at every possible point in the poem. Contrast is probably the most important feature of the rhetoric of *Beowulf.* The poet who fell heir to the Germanic poetic tradition became the possessor not only of a meter and a vocabulary and a stock of classic tales but also of a certain way of seeing and verbalizing the world in bold colors and sharp oppositions. The poem—indeed one could say the traditional style itself—explicitly and untiringly states and restates a code of truly heroic behavior. Such a code is easier to state than to live up to, of course, and the conventional language always has pulling against it a real sense of moral strain. Thus, over and over again, a king will be called ring giver, protector of his subjects, friend to his people; but the king must constantly *will* to be these things. A warrior is said, over and over again, to be brave and tough and loyal, but the more he is called these names or applies them to himself in his boasting in the mead hall, the more he must feel the mounting pressure to validate the words through unmistakable action.

It seems likely that much of our feeling of this kind of constant tension stems from the poet's use of highly colored and abruptly polarized contrasts and negative examples. By such means the possibility of things being otherwise is always felt to be present. Thus we have mention in the poem not only of several good kings, but of the bad king, like Heremod, who hoards his wealth and murders his people; or of the disloyal kinsman, like Hrothulf, who plots against his uncle; or of the cowardly warrior, like the loudmouthed Unferth at the Danish court or like the Geats who run away to safety in the forest when Beowulf steps forward to challenge the dragon.

If we return to our small scale again, we can see how contrast works on the level of style in this last instance. The Geats' behavior is described in the following passage:

> Nealles him on heape   handgesteallan,
> æthelinga bearn,   ymbe gestodon
> hildecystum,   ac hy on holt bugon,
> ealdre burgan. (2596–99)

In no way did those hand comrades, those sons of noblemen, take their stand around him in formation—no, they fell back into the forest and protected their own lives.

The sentence puts in sharp juxtaposition the poet's painfully explicit statement of what they should have done, as aristocratic members of the comitatus sworn to stand by their lord in battle to the end, and his account of what they actually did. Here again the alliteration on *hildecystum* "military formations" and *holt* "forest" sharpens our sense of the alternatives: they have two directions to take, to stand and fight like men or to run off and save their own lives. Alternatives mean choice, and the many passages of this kind in the poem keep our awareness of the hero's freedom to make such a choice constantly alive.

Obviously it is not easy for any translator to preserve many of these small-scale rhetorical patterns, but the larger contrasts in the poem (as we will see later in more detail) are unmistakably plain in any translation. The glittering and joyous hall of the Danes is "not far as we measure miles" from the ghoulish horrors of the haunted mere where the Grendel race lurks; the blood-drenched destiny of Heorot in its future feuds is not far in years from the great banquet that celebrates Beowulf's present triumphs. Passage after passage takes pains to emphasize the cruel disparity between a character's expectations and his ultimate fate. In the first part of the poem, Beowulf in his youthful vigors is set in contrast with the venerable Hrothgar, and the second part of the poem sets the very old Beowulf in contrast with young Beowulf.

Perhaps these few examples will serve to suggest, even to the reader unfamiliar with the poem in the original, some of the ways in which the habitual style of *Beowulf* is closely related to the themes and "meanings" of the poem. While the poet's conventional language may seem to offer the audience continual reinforcement of its feelings of security and familiarity and to picture a world where we can be "assured of certain certainties," the same language is often used to hint bleakly at a world where threat, uncertainty, and violent change are always very near. As contexts and tones keep shifting in response to the main action of the poem, the invariable formulas that embody the heroic view of life now seem to take on some dimension of pathos or irony, even a kind of despair, where word and deed grow far apart, and now sound like trumpet calls when heroic action swells them into radiant truth. But always they ring like conscience in our ears.

❧ II ❧

BEOWULF IN DENMARK

THE INTRODUCTION OF THE HERO

As we have already noticed, *Beowulf* opens not with the expected mention of the hero but with the apparently irrelevant description of the mysterious coming of Scyld to the Danes and of his splendid funeral. In the context of the poem as a whole, however, this is an effective beginning. It is important for the poet to establish the antiquity and glory of the Danish dynasty to which Hrothgar belongs by telling us of Scyld, but beyond that he is also furnishing us here with a heroic paradigm, a role-model for the hero of the poem. If we look at Beowulf's own career, we notice that (at least from the Danes' point of view) he too arrives suddenly and unexpectedly from somewhere else to rescue them from calamity and to restore their kingdom to them before he goes away, never (so far as we are told in the poem) to return to Denmark. Furthermore, the poem ends with Beowulf's own great funeral which is very close to that of Scyld in its emotional tone. The majestic, almost mythical cycle of a hero's life and death, at the same time triumphant and tragic, is equally present in the small action and in the large. The mythical atmosphere of the Scyld episode accords with a little evidence from outside the poem that hints at some ancient ritual of fertility involving Scyld and/or his father Sceaf (a name meaning "sheaf"). Perhaps then the Scyld story, often called a prologue or proem, has a function a little like that of the prologue of an Elizabethan play in the way it briefly hints not only at the outline of the action to follow but at the emotions appropriate to that action.

We move then through the catalogue of Scyld's royal descendants, the Scyldings, to King Hrothgar and to the initial action of the poem proper, the building of the great hall Heorot. Because his success in warfare has caused Hrothgar's reputation to expand and his band of men to increase, he wishes now to make his achievement visible and tangible by building the greatest hall that men have ever heard of and dedicating it specifically to acts of giving and to the distributing to his people of all the wealth which generous God has given him. In this creative and munificent act and in the act of naming the hall ("he created the name Heorot"), Hrothgar is almost godlike; he truly makes a world. In the completed hall, treasure is dispensed as promised, while the scop sings of how the Almighty made the earth, placing sun and moon as lights for men and adding the beauty of limbs and leaves. Both light and song reflect the joy of a human community attuned to cosmic order: indeed the light of Heorot, as the poet tells us later, shone far out over many lands.

But from the beginning this flowering of joy and power stands surrounded by darker contrasts. Some day not too far in the future Heorot is fated to be burned in the fighting between Danes and Heathobards: "the hall towered high and wide-gabled: it waited for the hostile surgings of flame." But much closer at hand than this ultimate threat is the grim spirit who is listening in the darkness to the song of creation. Grendel suffers acute pain when he hears the loud joy in the hall, and it is this pain that drives him out to attack and destroy. The contrast between the joy inside the hall and the rage and grief outside is part of a set of contrasts which defines both the ideal of heroic society and the forces which oppose it.

Part of this definition is made clear when the poet goes on to describe Grendel's descent from Cain and, partly by the conventional language used, to associate both Cain and Grendel with the type of the exile "driven far away from mankind." If the Danish Scyldings exist within the ordered structure of a proud dynasty, a succession of mighty kings, what we are told of the race of Cain seems a deliberately blurred and jumbled parody of the very concept of dynasty: "from him [Cain] were born all misbegotten creatures, ogres and elves and hellspirits, and giants too who fought against God so long a time; He paid them back for that!" Whereas the Danish kings ruled ("held") their men in warm personal relationship, Grendel "held" only the moors and wilderness of the marshlands. As the account of the building of Heorot as "gold hall" has made clear, heroic civilization is entirely based on the creative act of giving within the framework of a communal "family." By the very fact of his descent from the first disrupter of the family group, the first slayer of kin, Grendel is barred from ever understanding this fact. Even though he is strong and has the power to invade Heorot, he can never draw near Hrothgar's gift throne like the other retainers.

Their symbolic nature thus quickly identified at the outset, the two conflicting forces of "Grendel" and "Heorot" are now brought together in the clash of action. And now the rhythm of abrupt change, which is to sound so often all through the poem, begins. For the Danes in Heorot the heights of joy become in an instant the depths of sorrow; the happy song of yesterday becomes the anguished lament, the "great morning song" of the tormented Danes when they find their hall ravaged by Grendel and their companions gone. The poet has explained Grendel's origin as one of the race of Cain to his audience but apparently not to the Danes, who now grope pathetically for some way of comprehending what has happened to them, as the days go by and the attacks continue. Grendel is obviously waging a perpetual feud against them, but, unlike any human antagonist, he scorns to pay any wergild for the men he has killed: "none of the wise men of the Danes had any reason to expect the shining remedy [gold] from that killer's hands!" The very absurdity of such an attempt to force Grendel into human categories leads us toward the truth. The ensuing lines show us Grendel as a monstrous "dark death shadow," prowling the misty moors in eternal night, far beyond man's ken. He is no man, but the enemy of mankind.

The poet's general purpose up to this point in the poem seems to have been first to create the impression of an immensely powerful nation (clearly the Scyld story plays a large part in this) and then to introduce an attacker who is capable of reducing that nation to utter helplessness. By such simple means the audience gains a vivid sense of a great space to be filled, of a power vacuum the dimensions of which shape in advance the dimensions of the hero who is to move into it. Even though Beowulf has not even been mentioned in the first 193 lines, we have really been talking indirectly of no one else, for heroic poetry has a single-minded tendency to convert all settings, events, and antagonists into forms of characterization of the central hero. All parts of the poem exist only to make plain the greatness of his action and the transcendent power of his will.

After describing the Danes' worship of heathen idols in their despair (a passage mentioned briefly in the first chapter as a possible interpolation), the poet gives a summary of Danish misery which we may quote at some length here, together with the lines which follow and introduce the hero:

> In this way the son of Healfdene [Hrothgar] brooded over the troubles of the time, but that wise man could not turn away the affliction. For the struggle that visited that nation was too unequal, too vicious and long-lasting, a harsh fated torment, greatest of night's evils. A brave man of the Geats, Hygelac's thane, heard of Grendel's deeds from his home; he was the strongest of all mankind at that time of this life, noble and endowed with special power. He ordered a stout wave-traveler made ready and said he intended to visit the king across the swan-road, since that famous prince needed men. (189–201)

Contrasts dominate this passage. From a stylistic point of view, the heavy rhetoric, with its many appositives, with which the Danes' plight is described, is distinctly different from the lighter style, with fewer variations, in the passage introducing Beowulf. In terms of meaning, the way even the possibility of action on Hrothgar's part against so overwhelming an antagonist is ruled out is set against the way Beowulf moves instantly into action. He no sooner hears the story than he orders a ship prepared for the journey, giving his explanation of where he is going only after he has issued the command. To put it another way, the contrast is between Hrothgar's mental sufferings and the hero's physical strength. Even though the mention of Beowulf's name is withheld until the hero identifies himself to the official who guards the door of Hrothgar's hall (line 343), in these first few lines we can have no doubt at all that we are seeing a hero, a man who carries wherever he goes the full freedom to act in defense of the human community.

The scenes that follow, up to the climactic moment when the Danes hand their hall over to Beowulf to defend, may be better understood by the reader if he considers them in terms of a kind of dramatic irony. The poet is presenting his hero to two audiences at the same time: to the audience listening to his poem and to the Danes that Beowulf meets. The first of these audiences must recognize as soon as possible that Beowulf is a true hero so that they will find a special pleasure in the experience of watching the faces of those who meet him for the first time. Indeed, from this point of view, one chief function of the vivid description of the voyage of Beowulf and his men to Denmark is to reinforce the initial impression of strength we were given when the hero was first introduced, and to expand it into an image of effortless and unstoppable power, as the hero's ship flies like a great bird swiftly and smoothly to the distant shore. This image is fresh in our minds when Beowulf is challenged by the Danish coast guard; we already know something the Dane has not yet discovered.

The relationship of Beowulf to the Danes is not without possible complications, as common sense alone would suggest. He must first of all persuade a proud and dignified people to grant him the chance to meet Grendel. He comes from another country—not a country hostile to Denmark, but still foreign and very probably less important—with a bold offer to do for the Danes what they so very clearly are unable to do for themselves. Ultimately he will face Grendel in physical combat, but only after he has successively come to terms with the coast guard, the herald at the door, Hrothgar, and Unferth. Consequently his heroic credentials must include not only the essential element of physical strength and determination we have noticed but also the knowledge of how to use words properly, how to be tactful and courteous without giving up any firmness, and how to judge the right moment to be self-assertive. Many a later romance was to use a series of challenges as a useful device for gradually revealing character, but rarely with the effectiveness and economy that we see in *Beowulf*. In the course of winning over the Danes, Beowulf wins us all over.

The Danish coast guard who stands by a wall and holds a mighty spear by his very role and posture projects a proud and hostile reaction to the arrival of the Geats. But he seems to realize quickly that there is something peculiar about these strangers; his speech of challenge reflects some bewilderment. People either come to Denmark with the full permission of the Danes, he announces sternly, or they sneak ashore secretly as spies. They never come, his long years of experience have taught him, the way these people come, fully armed and yet without any concealment or any fear. And we see the formal austerity of his speech falter a little when he comments parenthetically on the sheer size of one of the Geats—no hall-lounger, that one, but a fighter. It is evident that the heroic appearance of Beowulf has impressed this Dane, but much still depends on the nature of Beowulf's reply to his challenge.

The first mystery Beowulf must clear up is who they are, and "who they are" in heroic poetry is to a very great extent a matter of their family and clan relationships. He explains quickly that they are Geats and the men of Hygelac the king, and then mentions the name of his own father Ecgtheow, who lived long and was known to every wise man. The unspoken implication may be that the coast guard will have heard of Ecgtheow if he lays any claim to being well informed. But more important now is the motive for their coming. We have come, Beowulf says, to see your lord Hrothgar, protector of his people (an honorific phrase used here in tact rather than irony), in a loyal spirit. It is implied that the Geats recognize and share the coast guard's respectful attitude toward his own king.

But at this delicate point Beowulf is very careful not to push himself forward too fast. Instead, he asks the coast guard to help him with advice and information. Whatever suspicions the Danes may have, Beowulf declares that there is nothing whatever that is secret about his mission. The Geats have simply heard a rumor—and the coast guard will know whether there is any truth to it or not—that some kind of monster has been plaguing the Danes. At this point Beowulf does not offer himself in the role of monster-fighter. What he offers is a *plan* by which Hrothgar might defeat Grendel, if— and the cautious concession to fate is typical of this hero—Grendel is ever destined to be defeated. He does not give any details of the plan.

So amiable and deferential a reply simply disarms the Danish coast guard. This is what I hear in your words, he says, that this is a band of men loyal to my king. Then he not only offers to guide them to Heorot but volunteers to have his men guard their boat until they come back. And when he leaves them in sight of Heorot, he calls down God's blessing on all their future journeys.

Now polished metal glints and mail coats sing their shrill song of clashing rings, as the Geats march up the stone-paved street to the great hall, but this sudden display of martial power is kept always under strict discipline. In deference to heroic decorum, they lean their shields and spears against the wall and sit calmly waiting on the bench outside the door. The doorkeeper Wulfgar first notices their menacing weapons and then, on second glance, their moral qualities. He concludes at once that they are brave and noble, and that their mission to Hrothgar must have a good purpose.

Although we have not much evidence for it, something like a code of courtly etiquette must have existed in Anglo-Saxon times; it is unlikely that it sprang into existence only in the later Middle Ages. Wulgar seems to be the major-domo or herald of Hrothgar's court, and the scene where Beowulf meets him is perhaps to be regarded as a special kind of test in manners. Wulfgar's speeches are couched in formal and roundabout phrases, and full of honorific variations and appositives; it seems to be a courtier's language. The test is whether Beowulf too can speak this language. He speaks it so well that Wulfgar, after dutifully reporting the coming of the Geats to his king, immediately departs from formality to plead earnestly with Hrothgar to admit them to the hall.

In his turn, Hrothgar, if he is to show himself a good king, must know what goes on in the heroic world. If there is a small test here for him, he passes it, for he knows who Beowulf is, knew him as a boy, knew his father very well, and has already heard stories of the young man's great strength. He leaps instantly to the conclusion that God must have sent Beowulf to save the Danes from Grendel. His welcome is immediate and wholehearted. But the hero is not yet fully accepted, nor has he yet presented all his qualifications. Up until now he has shown himself modest and reserved. The extent of his potential for aggressive action has only been hinted at in physical descriptions and in the awed reactions of the Danes to his appearance. Now, however, it is time to provide more explicit evidence of his talents.

The crucial speech (lines 407–55) that Beowulf addresses to
Hrothgar after he enters the hall is made somewhat clearer if we
take it as an almost methodical series of answers to some important
unspoken questions, or as Beowulf's way of forestalling and coping
with possible doubts or objections. Let us now paraphrase the
speech, putting the hypothetical unspoken questions in parentheses.
(Who are you?) I am Hygelac's kinsman and retainer. (What have
you ever done?) I have undertaken many well-known adventures,
young as I am. (Why have you come here? Do you have any witnesses
to support your claims?) I heard about the "Grendel affair" and
the most reputable men in my country urged me to come here,
because they themselves had already been eyewitnesses when I
bound five giants and slaughtered sea monsters. (Do you realize that
you are in a Danish hall?) I now most reverently beg the prince of
the Bright-Danes, protector of the Scyldings, to grant me and my
men permission to cleanse Heorot. (Have you any idea what this
involves?) Yes, precisely. I already know that Grendel does not use
weapons and that I will have to wrestle with him. And I know that
Grendel will try to eat Geats just as he ate Danes, and maybe he
will eat me. If so, I know he will carry my body off, smack his lips
over it, devour my flesh, smear blood all over the moorlands. You
will not have to worry about the funeral arrangements, but you
might send my mail coat back to Hygelac. Things will turn out the
way they turn out.

One has the strong feeling at the end of this speech that Beowulf
knows more about his enemy than the Danes themselves do, and
that he is brave enough to look at the prospect of an unpleasant
death in a way so realistic and unflinching that he is able to make a
joke of it.

But, even though Hrothgar now accepts Beowulf's good intentions and confesses to him how helpless the Danes have been against
Grendel's attacks, there is still one test to come. And in this last test
some of our unspoken questions are now spoken, quite loudly, by
Unferth, who sits at the feet of the king. Unferth is a puzzling character to modern readers of the poem. He seems to have some kind
of semiofficial role at the court; at least he holds the title of *thyle,*
a confusing term whose equivalent also appears in Old Norse litera-

ture. No one is certain, however, just what a *thyle* is or does: he has been variously regarded as a special adviser to the king, an official speechmaker or orator, a court jester, even as a licensed insulter of guests. Unferth may be personally jealous of Beowulf's reputation, as the poet says, or he may be drunk, as Beowulf later proposes, or he may simply be doing his job, whether that job involves deliberately ruffling a guest's feathers to see how he will take it or whether it involves merely stirring up an amusing situation in order to entertain the court.

Yet, even if Unferth's own reasons for attacking Beowulf remain obscure to us, the poet's reasons for introducing the speech at this point are easier to see. Unferth's speech is not only the climax in the series of challenges offered to Beowulf, it is the one test that will permit and require the hero to take off all wraps of courtesy and give his challenger a stirringly heroic belt in the chops. For this to happen, Unferth's speech must be rude and aggravating, and it is. Unferth says that he has heard of some fellow named Beowulf, some bragging fool who once insisted on having a stupid long-distance swimming contest with a man named Breca and who was ignominiously beaten in it. Are you *that* Beowulf? We have heard, Unferth is implying, that you are quick to boast and to commit yourself to large and foolish projects, but you do not come through in the end. Unferth may not be the only Dane with such misgivings at this juncture.

After a little gentle mockery of Unferth's drunken talkativeness, Beowulf in his reply starts out to set the record straight on exactly what happened in the swim with Breca. The boast may have been a foolish one, he concedes, but that was because we were only boys engaging in friendly rivalry. We swam together until a storm came up to separate us, and I kept my eye on him as long as I could. Beowulf then tells of how he fought alone against the storm and how he battled the sea monsters which had been stirred up by the storm, all through one long and terrible night, until at last the morning light, God's bright beacon, showed him the land. This fight with the monsters is plainly a tremendous exploit, but the hero consistently attributes the fortunate outcome to some power outside himself.

Wyrd oft nereth
unfægne eorl, thonne his ellen deah. (172–73)

Fate often saves a man who is not doomed to die, when his courage is
good! The ambiguity we find in these lines runs through the poem,
as it runs through most heroic poetry. Fortune favors the brave, and
God helps those who help themselves, and only those: yet the heroes
know better than anyone their ultimate dependence on luck and
chance and the mysterious hand of the gods. As Beowulf's reply de-
velops in eloquence and rhetorical momentum, it becomes more
of an answer than Unferth deserved, for it pictures in the symbol of
the sea that great Unknowable that both resists and carries to
safety the resolute hero. Indeed we forget about Unferth under
the spell of this assertion of heroic vigor and faith.

But in the end Beowulf does bring his artillery to bear on Unferth,
because it is evidently expected of him. In this verbal battle, so much
like those later Scottish contests of abuse known as flytings, insult
can only be matched by insult. In the closing lines of the speech,
Unferth is demolished. I never heard, says Beowulf, that you ever
did anything like that, Unferth. The only thing I ever heard about
you was that you killed your brothers (and for that crime you will
suffer in hell, clever as you are). No, if you were as brave as you
claim to be, Grendel would never have caused so much trouble here;
but he has found out by now that he has nothing to fear from the
Danes. And now I'll show him what a Geat's courage is like!

In this last remark, Beowulf is surely being more plain-spoken
about the Danes' inability to drive away their invader than we might
think prudent, but his ringing scorn and self-assertion are unmistakably what are demanded here. The king is overjoyed to hear
how determined this young stranger is. Unferth's own reaction is
not recorded, but later in the poem he lends Beowulf his sword
and is courteously thanked for it.

Yet it may be that the harmony of the community has been put to
a severe strain in this exchange, and perhaps that is why a scene of
feasting follows, with the focus on Queen Wealhtheow, the peace-
maker, making the ceremonial rounds with the loving cup. When
she brings the cup to Beowulf, he makes his formal boast or vow

—what the Anglo-Saxons called a *beot*—in which he declares that he will completely carry out the will of the Danish people or die. The allusion to the fusing of his will and theirs is significant. Beowulf has now become entirely a part of the society in the hall. King Hrothgar, as he leaves now to go to the *bur* where he sleeps, says that he has never before turned his hall over to another man, but now he gives it over to Beowulf to "have and to hold."

To sum up then, we have seen that the greatest part of the first 700 lines of the poem have been devoted to the gradual revelation of the nature of a particular kind of hero. Immense physical strength is always a part of Beowulf's presence: it flashes out briefly in the description of the masterful voyage, in the armed march up to the hall, in the sudden hammering energy of the hero's laconic accounts of his previous exploits. Yet we are to be as much impressed by the intelligent discipline that controls and directs that strength, a discipline evident in his deep respect for Hrothgar as leader of a great civilization, in the instinctive tact of his encounters with the Danes, and in his clear-eyed estimate of possible danger and death. In such a hero as this, self-affirmation and altruistic idealism are hardly separable from each other. Beowulf is the heroic individual who stands ready to commit all his mysterious power to the defense of society.

THE FIGHT WITH GRENDEL

Grendel, the monster that attacks Heorot and devours its Danish defenders, is never described in precise physical detail, perhaps because the original audience was familiar with the traditional appearance of such creatures or perhaps simply because the very vagueness of outline was a time-tested way of creating the desired effect of horror. Typical is the dim glimpse of Grendel and his mother which the Danes pass on to Hrothgar, who tells Beowulf:

> I have heard my people living in the land, the hall-dwellers, say that they saw two such great stalkers of the wasteland, alien creatures, guarding the moors. So far as they could make out, one of them was in the shape of a woman; the other misbegotten thing roamed the paths of exile in a man's shape, but bigger than any man—people called him Grendel in the old days.

In the later Scandinavian analogues of the story told in *Beowulf*, the monster is either a (male or female) troll, that is to say, a supernatural creature of human shape living in or near water, or he is a walking "undead" corpse, like the Caribbean zombie. Because it turns out to be apparently necessary for Beowulf to cut off the head of the already lifeless Grendel in the cave, this action has been viewed as the final ritual killing of an "undead" creature, like the driving of a stake through a vampire's heart, but most of the evidence indicates that the Grendel of *Beowulf* was a water-haunting troll.

For one thing, several Anglo-Saxon legal documents mention Grendel (or conceivably "a grendel," if it is taken as a common noun). Typical of these is a charter dated 708, which traces a boundary line "from Grendel's pit to the willow mere, from the willow mere into the red bog . . . from the ditch to the black pool, from the pool along the Piddle brook into the marsh and from the marsh back into Grendel's pit." [1] Here "Grendel's pit" is probably a deep water-filled hole in marshy country. Ancient superstitious fears of such uncanny places seem to play an important part in the dark terror associated with the Grendel race in *Beowulf*. The same primitive level of emotion can also be seen in one of the simpler folk tales which bears some resemblance to the Grendel story, the tale known as "The Hand and the Child," where a great demon arm reaches into a house by night to seize a child, until at last a hero grasps the arm and wrenches it off. Grendel too seems to be such a night bogy, persistently connected with darkness and mist.

As we have already seen, however, the poet of *Beowulf* has superimposed on this ancient demon of the swamps the story of his descent from Cain, together with the social and theological implications that go with it. Grendel bears both the mark of Cain and the wrath of God. He is sometimes regarded as an exile banished to the wilderness for brother-murder, like any Anglo-Saxon outlaw. His home in the foul pool is sometimes described as that hell on earth to which Cain was driven. None of the parallel stories in the sagas and folk tales have this important dimension of meaning. By making use of it, *Beowulf* can enter the realm of universal myth.

In the shadowy mere we can glimpse the blackness of ultimate evil, and a slouching brute of a troll becomes God's adversary.

But it would be imprudent to carry these theological implications further than the poet himself carries them. Whatever rich aroma Grendel may bring with him from his swamps, it is not the familiar stench of brimstone, for he is not a devil. If he eats men, he does not tempt them or try to destroy their souls. Nor, in his attacks on the hall, is he acting as the agent of God's retribution (as some have gone so far as to suggest), for the Danes have done no wrong.

From a slightly different point of view, what Grendel seems to represent is a rather complex objectification of antiheroic and anti-social forces intimately related by opposition to the positive heroic and social values of the poem, especially as they are embodied in the hero himself. Like Beowulf, Grendel is immensely strong, but his strength runs wild, beyond any rational control or constraint. Grendel's savage condition is hinted at even in the way Hrothgar's people speak of the two shadowy monsters they have seen—*like* a woman, or *in the shape of* a man. If Grendel has had originally a human kind of strength like Cain's, it has now blurred and become almost unrecognizable: he is a disturbingly alien creature who will no longer fit our familiar categories. But he is never totally un-recognizable. The poem succeeds in giving the figure of Grendel its memorable power precisely by keeping him flickering in that half world on the edge of the human, *manncynne fram,* far out away from mankind, and yet part of mankind. In his dull-wittedness, his tireless rage for destructive chaos, his massive rejection of com-munity, he is in direct contrast with Beowulf; but Grendel's hot animal vitality is only a twisted form of the raw energy that fuels Beowulf's own achievements. And Grendel's mother's single-minded passion for revenge when her son has been killed differs hardly at all from that fierce clan loyalty that upholds (and destroys) human societies. Indeed from this point of view it will be seen that the poem offers the modern reader familiar with Freudian theory the tempting conception of the monsters as embodiments of unconscious drives and the ravening id.

If Grendel shares the gift of physical strength with Beowulf, he is differentiated from the hero by his lack of intelligence more than by anything else. Perhaps intelligence is not as good a word to use here as awareness, almost a religious recognition of forces beyond oneself. We can see Grendel's peculiar stupidity very well in the scene when he approaches Heorot and the waiting Beowulf, after Hrothgar and the Danes have left the hall. It is interesting to notice how we are placed inside Grendel's mind before and during the fight with Beowulf; clearly the poet wants to record the monster's reactions. Grendel does not know what awaits him in the hall, but he thinks he does. The poet stresses his expectations and intentions as he bursts open the door and rushes into the hall. His fiery eyes roll gluttonously over the sleeping forms of the men in the hall, and he laughs in triumph as he moves forward and horribly devours one man.

Beowulf has been lying still, apparently studying the behavior of the monster. And now Grendel reaches out toward him. Since we have already been placed inside Grendel's consciousness, we are given a vivid sense of his instant reaction to the crushing grip of Beowulf's hand. To the extent that it is a battle of wills, the fight is simply over in the first second: Grendel reaches the immediate decision to flee and hide in the deepest part of his underwater domain. But he is terrified at being frustrated in these intentions, he cannot pull away with all his strength, until at last his panic rises to such a peak that he seems to wrench himself away from his own arm, leaving it in the hero's grasp. "I couldn't hold him," Beowulf explains to Hrothgar afterwards, "he was just too mighty at running away." All through the entire scene the contrast is maintained between Grendel and Beowulf, the hero who is aware of Grendel's coming and secure in his faith that God will decide the outcome of the fight, who watches Grendel's approach coolly, and who finally perhaps merely allows Grendel to defeat himself.

The poet has suffered some criticism for the way he has chosen to present the fight with Grendel, accompanied as it is with a good deal of commentary on the action and some rapidly shifting points of view. If we try to accept the passage as it is, however, we can see which themes the poet particularly wants to stress here, and we may come to realize how intensely symbolic the poem really is. The long and careful revelation of the hero to the Danes and to the audience of the poem that we have been tracing reaches one climax, as we have seen, when Beowulf accepts title to the hall for the night and makes his vow to defend it. Rather than stand in any kind of opposition to him, all Danish civilization has voluntarily consented to let Beowulf stand as its champion, and of course that is Beowulf's own wish as well. Thus it is a combined will, massed and focused, that is directed against Grendel when he comes to Heorot. On the other side, the poet's heavy emphasis on Grendel's gloating expectations makes the shock of the two touching hands the more dramatic, since it is the collision of two such tremendous wills. Beowulf's fearless handclasp is the final revelation of his heroic resolution, and seen from this point of view, Grendel is only the last in a series of challengers. Beowulf's victory is instantaneous and unqualified. All the strength of will that Grendel possesses crumbles, recoils on itself and is redirected *utweard,* outward, away from the hall's defender.

By now shifting our attention away from any actual description of this encounter, once we have been brought to grasp its symbolic implications, the poet can deepen our understanding by showing us a spectrum of degrees of comprehension of what the fight "means." We move out now to see the fight from the point of view of the Danes outside Heorot who wonder in their terror if their beloved hall can possibly withstand the battering it is undergoing; from the point of view of the wise designers of the hall who had never conceived of the stresses produced by such a fight; from the point of Beowulf's own Geats inside the hall, who staunchly draw swords to defend their master, unaware that swords cannot harm Grendel, because he has put a spell on them, and doubtless also unaware of the sheer panic Grendel is feeling. And always we have the point of view of the omniscient poet, who speaks with the assurance of fate itself: Grendel will be forced to die miserably; he is God's enemy; he will flee now to his joyless home. And the poet's voice authoritatively announces the victory of Beowulf in all its dimensions (lines 823 ff.): the will of the Danes is now carried out; the hall is cleansed; the Geat has fulfilled his vow to the Danes: and the indisputable proof of it all is now to be seen—"Grendel's grasp all together, hand, arm, and shoulder, under the spacious roof." And in the morning the Danes find further proof when they follow Grendel's tracks to the mere, the waves of which are now surging with hot blood.

Their relief and triumph now find expression in the release of exuberant energy. The skylarking Danes race their horses on the ride back from the mere, and their scop begins at once to search his hoard of heroic legends for comparisons to place beside Beowulf's great action. In a strange way, the same essential energy is manifest in the plunging reckless horses and the skilled fingers on the harp-strings. Beowulf has freed the Danes, after their agonies of blocked action, and allowed them to soar into singing strength again. And their burst of song carries Beowulf up into the company of a great hero like Sigemund, who earned his immortal fame by going alone to kill a mighty dragon. Sigemund used his gift of strength well, while Heremod, an ancient king of the Danes, had turned his gift of strength against his people, and tragedy had resulted. The contrastive rhetoric in the use of a positive and negative example is typical.

Hrothgar's reaction to the victory takes another form, a form quite characteristic of this majestically sententious patriarch. As he walks forward to look at Grendel's arm nailed up against the towering golden roof of his hall, he sees the miracle-working hand of God in his deliverance from despair. Only through God's help has Beowulf succeeded in doing what none of the Danes could do. And the old king turns gratefully to Beowulf and wishes to love him as a son, to adopt him forthwith into a new and intimate relationship. Beowulf's reply is attractively modest and deprecatory. He wishes Hrothgar had been there to watch Grendel in the fight; he is a little disappointed that he let the monster escape; and he too ends by redirecting attention to the great claw. And now Unferth looks at the monstrous hand with its steel-sharp fingers, and holds his tongue this time. All the verbiage, the challenges and claims and boasts that went before, have been superseded by this hand, and by the greater hand that bested it.

THE BANQUET INTERLUDE

Beowulf's defeat of Grendel and the chaotic forces he represents is itself something of an act of creation, for through it human community is reasserted and re-established. At this point, many traditional images of order and harmony flood into the poem, the most significant of them being the great victory feast held in Heorot. Before the feast can take place, Heorot must first be restored and redecorated, and many busy human hands (a contrast with Grendel's dead hand is apparent) cover the walls with tapestries. The rituals of feasting and the ceremonial pouring of drink follow. So great is the harmony that even Hrothgar and his nephew Hrothulf drink together, the poet tells us, adding that Heorot was then filled with friends and none of the Scyldings was practicing any treachery. Then marvelous gifts are brought out to be presented to Beowulf and his Geats before the eyes of the admiring crowd. Then the court poet sets about entertaining the happy feasters with an old lay of King Finn of the Frisians and how he waged a feud against the Danes but was defeated in the end.

It is all a little overdone, and the poet knows it. He knows, and the audience knows, that Hrothulf will one day practice treachery, and that men should never allow their feelings of exultation to lead them to relax their caution. Anyone who lives any length of time in this world in these hard days, he murmurs softly at the end of the presentation of gifts, will have to accept much that he likes and much that he doesn't. Life is not all joy, and it is desperately unstable. The foreground scene of rejoicing is real enough, but another dimension of reality is hinted at more and more strongly as the banquet goes on. The two points of view are nowhere more clearly seen than in the Finn tale which is sung in the hall.

Unfortunately for us, this story is told so elliptically and allusively, evidently to an audience capable of responding to slight hints by reconstructing the familiar story, that it offers serious problems in interpretation; even the early scribes seem to have been confused by the episode, to judge from some peculiar readings. Yet great expressive power remains in the passage, and indeed the power lies precisely in this very density and economy, in the bold way the poet trims his story down so as to focus attention on those who suffer most from the ironies of human passions.

In brief, the story (with a little background filled in) runs like this. King Hnæf of the Danes, with a band of his men, travels to visit his sister Hildeburh, who is the wife of King Finn of the Frisians. The visiting Danes are treacherously attacked at night by the Frisians (or perhaps by their allies the Jutes). Hnæf is killed and his second-in-command Hengest takes over. Hard fighting apparently ends in a draw, with both sides now too weak to win a victory. Finn and Hengest then negotiate a complicated peace treaty whereby the Danes and Frisians are to share a hall, the Danes swearing temporary allegiance to Finn, and the Frisians under a strict oath to refrain from jeering at the Danes for following their own king's slayer. After a funeral pyre disposes of the dead of both sides, Hengest and his men spend the winter at Finn's hall (since voyages were not ordinarily attempted in the winter), Hengest silently longing for a chance to gain vengeance. When spring comes, the feud explodes again (exactly how this comes about is not made clear), and the Danes take drastic revenge by killing Finn, plundering his hall, and taking his Danish widow Hildeburh back to Denmark with them in triumph.

This is a good story, and it could be effectively told in more ways than one. It is in fact told in a quite different way in a fragment of heroic verse known as *The Fight at Finnsburg,* which describes the first night attack on the Danes. This fragment is a superbly exciting narrative, with full stress on reckless unthinking action and the absolute courage of the heroic defenders of the hall. But the *Beowulf* poet seems interested in looking beyond such furious drives of violence and hatred to their ultimate effects on the participants. Thus he begins the episode by showing us Hildeburh the queen in the dawn after that first attack, as she comes to realize in the growing light that she has lost a brother (Hnæf) on the Danish side and a son on the Frisian side. However the feud may have started and whoever finally "wins" it, Hildeburh is a certain loser. She had indeed good reason to lament destiny, the poet observes with quiet feeling, when morning came and under the sky she could see the evil slaughter of kinsmen, in that very place where she had once known the greatest joy in the world. All she can do now is go through the hollow rite of the funeral, ordering her son's body to be placed on the pyre alongside the body of his uncle and chanting her sorrow as the fire, greediest of spirits, devours the dead of both nations. In such a context of grief and loss, the fire is at once part of Hildeburh's agony and part of the poet's unspoken judgment on the feud as cause of such suffering and waste.

Hengest, the other figure studied by the *Beowulf* poet, also suffers intensely, though from a different cause. Probably out of consideration for his own men's welfare and safety, he is compelled to violate every heroic instinct by swearing oaths of allegiance to the hated Finn who is responsible for the death of the Danish king. Not only that, he is also obliged to live with Finn for many months, pretending to be his loyal subject and taking part in the ring-giving ceremonies of the court. The dilemma of conflicting obligations paralyzes all action, at least until spring comes and travel is again possible. Images of winter storm and ice-locked waves objectify Hengest's mental state all through that "slaughter-stained winter."

Then someone apparently gives Hengest a sword, perhaps King Hnæf's sword, as a reminder of his duty, and the Frisians are at last attacked. It is very tempting for a modern reader to see in Hengest a Hamletlike reluctance to rush toward vengeance, but there is too little evidence in the text to support the assumption. Furthermore, we do not know what Hengest feels after the final battle begins, for this fight is told in a markedly impersonal way. It is "sword evil" that kills Finn; "restless spirit" can no longer hold itself back; the hall is stained red, Finn slain, the queen taken—all passive constructions. This way of rendering the action tends to suggest a blind, runaway force of destruction that engulfs and transcends the individual participants, the same kind of force symbolized earlier in the episode by the image of fire. Surely the happy ending here is cruelly darkened by irony, when Hildeburh simply becomes one more item of loot from Finn's hall. Having succeeded in killing her husband, the Danes now take her home "to her people."

It is quite true that after the scop ends his tale of Finn the merriment in Heorot becomes even more uproarious. To the Danish audience in the hall, the story has been an agreeably familiar celebration of the triumph of Danish vengeance and probably even seems to them an appropriate analogue to Beowulf's victory over Grendel. But the poet is directing some dimension of meaning over their heads to his own audience. As we have seen, the poet, by the way he tells the story, makes successful vengeance seem less important than the helpless suffering brought about by such violent disruption of the human community. He reminds us, moreover, of the fearful suddenness with which a scene of peace—it was Hildeburh's family reunion—can in a flash become a scene of massacre. If the Finn episode is in its way, then, a general comment on the constant threat of disastrous change in heroic life, is it also related more specifically to other events in the poem? Most careful readers have felt that it is.

Immediately after the end of the Finn tale, Queen Wealhtheow walks forward majestically to where Hrothgar and his nephew Hrothulf are sitting with Unferth. Uncle and nephew are true to each other, the poet is at pains to tell us, and they all trust Unferth, even though he has not been honorable to his kinsmen in the play of sword edges (a very Anglo-Saxon way of alluding to Unferth's murder of brother or brothers). We have no way of being sure just what Unferth has to do with the other two, but we do know from sources outside the poem that Hrothulf will some day turn against his uncle (as nephews in Germanic literature frequently did), and it becomes clear that the queen already fears this may happen. Why else would she make a point of urging her husband Hrothgar to leave Heorot to his sons when he dies? Why else would she tell us how very confident she is that Hrothulf will remember all they have done for him and that he will treat her sons kindly when they grow up? And later why else does she beg the visiting Beowulf to treat her sons well?

Since the poet could count on his audience knowing the rest of the story, he is able to charge the scene with intense dramatic irony, simply by presenting Queen Wealhtheow's anxious and urgent pleas for the maintenance of harmonious relationships. And suddenly a further pattern of meaning leaps into focus. As Hildeburh was, Wealhtheow will be. Now Wealhtheow has her family together in a peaceful hall, but Hildeburh too knew her greatest joys just the night before the slaughter of her loved ones began.

From this point of view, then, the Finn story is the powerful first statement of a genuinely tragic theme that becomes more and more prominent as the poem moves on. We learn later from Beowulf of a second threat to the harmony of Heorot, when he tells his king, Hygelac, of the proposed marriage of Hrothgar's daughter Freawaru to young Ingeld of the Heathobards. It is made very plain that Freawaru too will fit the tragic pattern of Hildeburh and Wealhtheow: her attempt to bring peace between feuding tribes will end in heartbreak.

Perhaps the joyful security of the lighted and festive hall, newly restored to its proper function after twelve years of Grendel's depredations, now seems all the more poignantly valuable, when we are brought to realize how short-lived human joy must always be. Short-lived indeed; the brevity of joy could hardly be more strikingly dramatized than by what follows in the poem, the wholly unexpected attack of Grendel's mother on the hall after only a few hours of blissful respite. "Sorrow is renewed for the people of the Danes," mourns Hrothgar. In the world of *Beowulf,* sorrow is unfailingly renewed.

The Fight with Grendel's Mother

The poet obviously made no attempt earlier to surprise us in the lines leading up to and including the first fight with Grendel. We were genuinely interested in the revelation of Beowulf's heroic nature, but the issue of the fight was never much in doubt. Indeed, before Grendel even appears at the hall where Beowulf is waiting, the poet is telling us that God granted Beowulf and the Geats success in this conflict, and certainly Grendel's undisguised terror from the moment he touches Beowulf ends all suspense about the eventual outcome of that struggle. But Grendel's mother is another matter. She breaks into the poem as she breaks into the hall, out of nowhere, for she has never even been mentioned before. The shock —and perhaps the silent rebuke to human overconfidence—is the greater.

To take her somewhat abstractly, Grendel's mother is a restating of the principle of evil in somewhat modified form. It is certainly true that she is primarily what Grendel is. One may even wish to regard her as something in Grendel, or of Grendel, that is still alive and that comes back to attack humanity, a merely scotched snake still writhing. But now the opposition of symbolic forces that we saw in the Grendel-Heorot contrast has developed new complications. Grendel's mother has an authentic motive for coming to Heorot and carrying off the Danish counselor Æschere: she must take revenge for her son's death. We may never have quite understood what lay behind her son's monstrous rages—perhaps we were not meant to—but the original audience knew all about the principle of a family's obligation to take vengeance. Such a clear motive may make Grendel's mother not only less mysterious but perhaps even less blackly evil. In any event, she is certainly not given the thick overlay of theological guilt (in phrases like "God's adversary," "bearing God's anger," and so on) that is applied to Grendel. The motive of vengeance, moreover, associates the "outside" monsters more closely with the "inside" manifestations of purely human violence that we see in the blood feuds. Thus moral issues may come to seem less clear-cut, and some have offered this fact as an explanation for the much more difficult struggle that Beowulf has with the female member of the race of Cain. Possibly so, though it is obvious that the poet would have to make the fight somewhat more difficult if only to avoid an anticlimax.

Probably the most important aspect of the second fight is its location at the bottom of the haunted mere where the Grendel race lives. The suddenness of the coming of Grendel's mother is matched by the suddenness with which, for the first time, we are forced to shift our attention out from Heorot to quite a different world. The more the great metaphors of order and happiness are developed in the banquet scene, the sharper the contrast provided by the chill horrors of that evil center out beyond the circle of light.

In a famous passage Hrothgar, now recalling that his Danes had once reported seeing two great border-stalkers, describes to Beowulf the place where they live:

It is a hidden land they defend—wolf slopes, windswept cliffs, a treacherous marsh, where a mountain stream comes down under the darkness of cliffs, water vanishing under earth. That mere stands not far from here, as we measure miles. Frost-coated groves hang over it; a firm-rooted forest stands guard over the water. There every night you can see a deadly wonder—fire on the water. No one of the sons of men lives so old and wise that he knows the bottom of it. Even if the stiff-horned hart, that pacer of the wilds, drove for this forest hard running with hounds at his heels, he would sooner give up life on the shore than enter there to save his neck. That is no decent place! From it tumultuous waves boil up dark to the clouds, driven by wind and foul weather, till air darkens and the sky streams tears. (1357–76)

The dark power rooted in this tortured place wards off all approach, protecting itself not only by wolves and wild terrain and storms but by the unnatural combinations of elements that keep the mere unknown and inaccessible and violently repel the hunted deer whose instinct leads it to prefer death to any contact with so evil a region. If we once saw Heorot, the hall of men, exercising its attraction for Grendel, this unholy mere repels men with such terrific force that even the march to its shores is represented as a striking feat of courage by Hrothgar and his Danes. A descent into its depths seems unimaginable.

Grendel's mother is closely linked with this mere in several ways. Such epithets as "she-wolf of the sea," "accursed creature of the depths," or "mighty mere-woman" are often applied to her. Furthermore, we get our first good look at her, not when she makes her hasty raid on Heorot, but when she is fighting in the water and in the strange firelit hall at the bottom of the mere where she lives.

All these things make the "meaning" of the evil that Beowulf must combat in this encounter rather complicated. The evil is both human and nonhuman, but with a strong shading toward the nonhuman. The Cain story suggests the origin of the evil in some primeval projection outward of man's violence, but the description of the mere, with its loathsome swarm of sea monsters, implies some long process during which such human evil has become twisted into the hallucinatory and bestial. If Grendel's mother has the understandable human motive of revenge, she is also represented as purely animal in appearance and behavior, much more of an animal than her son, and we are given almost no information on her mental processes.

If the poet gives more prominence to such alien and nonhuman aspects of the enemy in this second fight, he also seems to weave an especially appropriate web of symbols about his hero to fit him for the new contest. Perhaps it could all be summed up by saying that Beowulf is made more human, is represented more emphatically as a man related to other men.

After Hrothgar has described the mere in terrifying terms and invited Beowulf to try his strength there, Beowulf shows no reaction to the frightening picture that has been drawn, but rather he responds directly to Hrothgar's emotional condition. He sees that the king is upset and despairing, and consequently he must take care to remind him at just this time of the fundamentals of the heroic life:

> O wise man, do not grieve! It is better for everyone to avenge a friend than to mourn a great deal. Each one of us has to live until the end of life in this world. If we can, we should earn fame before death, for that is the best thing a warrior can have after he is dead. Stand up now, guardian of the kingdom, and let us go quickly and look at the track of Grendel's mother. I promise you this: she will never escape to safety, not in the embrace of the earth, not in the mountain forest, not at the bottom of the sea, no matter where she may go!

Since hope and meaning in the heroic life are found only in action, the only possible response to the terror of the mere is to act against it. Only after Beowulf has persuaded Hrothgar to take the symbolic action of rising to his feet can he offer the king his promise. The last sentence quoted shows that Beowulf did indeed notice the details of Hrothgar's description, but now these details form part of a chanted expression of human determination hurled like a challenge into the darkest stronghold of the evil forces.

Beowulf was without sword or armor when he met Grendel, but he must prepare elaborately for the second fight. These items of his equipment are not really part of himself: made by other hands or borrowed (like Unferth's sword) from other men, they are necessarily symbols of human interdependence. Traditional phrases crowd into the description to remind us that his mail shirt was "woven by hands" and that ancient smiths once labored lovingly over the forging of his helmet. We may remember these phrases and their delicate suggestion of many men's hands when the vicious attack by Grendel's mother comes: "rings stood stout guard outside—she could not pierce that war shirt, that interlocked limb protector, with her terrible fingers." Moreover, although it is quite conventional in Germanic poetry to grant a certain degree of personification to weapons (to give names to swords, for example), the description of Beowulf's arms here seems to contain an unusual amount of it. The mail shirt is to "make trial of swimming" and the helmet will wear its rich adornments to the sea bottom. Unferth's sword Hrunting, like a hero, has a name and a past reputation, and can be counted on to perform courageously. They are all good companions to have. Beowulf will not dive down through the waters of the mere entirely alone.

A point essentially the same is also made by the speech Beowulf delivers just before he dives into the water. He does not even mention the mere or its inhabitants, but is wholly concerned with important relationships among human beings. He reminds Hrothgar first of the intimate father-son relationship that has grown between them and then calls on him to honor the obligation in the event of the hero's death in the fight by serving as the *mundbora,* the legal protector, to his Geatish followers, by forwarding the treasures to Hygelac so that he will know what a generous king Hrothgar is, and by giving Unferth a sword to replace the one he has lent Beowulf. Here, as so often in the latter third of the poem, attention is fixed equally on human ties of love and duty and on the possibility, calmly and realistically accepted, of imminent death. The two themes seem to go together in *Beowulf.*

When Beowulf enters the mere and begins to swim toward the bottom, Grendel's mother recognizes that an important representative of the human race has entered the "country of alien creatures." Even from her dim point of view, issues have been clearly drawn, and the result for many lines is brilliant narrative action.

In this unexplored new world, Beowulf has a series of crucial and traumatic discoveries to make. He finds out first the immense strength of the enemy; this is no easily cowed Grendel he is fighting. The she-monster seizes him and carries him to her hall, the hero helpless and unable to wield his sword; only his armor protects him against the tusks of the swarming sea monsters. Dazed, he finds himself in a mysterious hall where water cannot enter, lit by eerie firelight. At length he makes out the figure of the monster. Rushing furiously toward her with his sword, again he learns something new: the sword is quite useless, its renowned edge failing him when he needs it. Now Beowulf hurls the sword away and trusts once more in the strength of his hands, but he is no match for Grendel's mother in wrestling. She scrambles up from a fall to squat on his chest, stabbing at his mail shirt with her dagger.

The hero would surely have perished at this point, the poet tells us, if his armor had not given him help and if God had not granted him victory and if he had not managed to stand up. All these ifs combine to form the same kind of ambiguity we saw earlier in the account of the swim with Breca. Again the point is made that God and luck do indeed work for the hero, but only after he has shown himself to be a hero through his own actions. If he does this, something then comes, like the gift of grace. Its coming is perhaps represented in this passage by Beowulf's sudden glimpse of a great, giant sword hanging on the wall. God must have shown him the sword (so Beowulf later tells Hrothgar), but only Beowulf could lift it and strike with it as he does, cutting through the monster's neck with a single tremendous blow. Light flashes out, like the bright light of the sun, "heaven's candle," shining down from the sky. If this is a sign, Beowulf does not pause to reflect on it, but moves along the wall in a search for Grendel's body. As we saw earlier, the total cleansing of the mere seems to require the ritual killing of Grendel. There is a faint irony in this passage, for Grendel had so often come to Heorot to seize men sleeping in their beds, and now Beowulf comes upon the monster in his own hall and his own bed. The corpse leaps in the air as Beowulf beheads Grendel with his own sword.

In *Beowulf,* as in other versions of the Bear's Son tale, watchers at the surface seeing blood in the water conclude that the hero has been killed and abandon their vigil. Here the Danes, whose inactivity all through this scene has been used by the poet to make a strong contrast with Beowulf's strenuous actions, decide to go back to Heorot. Beowulf's own Geats stay, heartsick, looking hopelessly at the water.

It is quite possible that a Christian audience would have been reminded at this point of Jesus' disciples after the Crucifixion. Indeed, on a broader scale, the whole pattern of action in Beowulf's descent into the evil mere and his triumphant return may have seemed to such an audience reminiscent of the enormously popular medieval story of the Harrowing of Hell, which tells of Christ's descent into hell after dying on the cross to release the patriarchs from bondage and to lead them back to heaven. We would be unwise, however, to draw from such a similarity—if indeed it is one—the simplistic conclusion that Beowulf is Christ. The theme of the hero's descent into a death world is widespread and antedates Christianity, as, for example, in the Greek myth of Orpheus and Eurydice. Indeed, it seems to be an important motif in such epics as *Gilgamesh* and the *Odyssey.*

It is evident that the despairing Geats feel that only a miracle will restore Beowulf to them. And at this very point a miracle is described, as we see the giant sword that Beowulf used to kill the monsters melting away in the poison of their blood until only the hilt is left.

> That was a great wonder, that it all melted just like ice, whenever the Father eases the frost-fetter and slackens the ropes that bind the waters, He who has power over all times and seasons. He is true Measurer of things. (1605–11)

The simile of ice (it might be noted parenthetically that similes are extremely rare in Old English poetry) carries us from the miracle of the sword's melting, which is the last perceptible manifestation of demonic power, to the miracle of ice melting, as it does every spring in the orderly cycle of divine process. The allusion to God's ultimate ordering power breaks in like the sudden gleam of light after the killing of Grendel's mother, in sign of the fact that by his heroic act Beowulf has cleansed the mere-world and restored it to a place in the world of ordered nature.

> The swirl of waves was wholly cleansed, and those great dwellings, when that alien spirit gave up life-days and this fleeting world. (1620–22)

Just as Beowulf left a world of men to enter the unnatural mere alone, moving out of a web of human relationships into the unknown, so he now returns to a world of men, as his devoted followers rush to greet him. The way an Old English poet can underline a theme subtly by using the traditional variational style is well illustrated in this passage, where the poet selects phrases that keep reminding us, on almost a subliminal level, of the bonds between men. Beowulf is called "protector of seafarers," "lord of men," and "prince of thanes," at the same time that actions and gestures dramatize the affectionate reunion. His followers thank God for Beowulf's safety; they loosen his helmet and armor and volunteer to carry the great burden of Grendel's head, which Beowulf has brought back as a trophy. Leader and men are reunited in meaningful cooperation as they march back to Heorot, laboring under the weight of the head.

Heroic achievement in *Beowulf* is both the single exploit of the individual and the knitting back together of a community that is the desired result of such an exploit. A proud and exultant group of men arrive at Heorot:

> Men bold as kings carried the head away from the sea cliff, each of the gallant men staggering under the load; it took four men to bear with heavy labor Grendel's head on a spear to the gold hall, until at last fourteen brave war-keen Geats came striding up to the hall; the lord of men walked brave in the midst of his men across the fields by the mead hall. Then the prince of thanes entered the hall, a man who had shown his bravery, now shining with glory, a battle-fierce fighter, to greet Hrothgar. Grendel's head was hauled by the hair onto the hall floor where men were drinking—appalling to the

warriors and the lady with them, a fantastic sight. The men looked at it. (1635–50)

The usual rhetoric of contrast demands that the Danes in Heorot must play again, as they did on the mere's edge, the role of those who look, feel, and do not act. But they are not condemned by the poet for not being Beowulf. However grossly, even comically incongrous the giant head may appear in the midst of Heorot's decorous rituals, it was precisely to save those rituals that Beowulf did what he did. Now the hero (a little out of breath) admits to the king that the fight gave him a lot of trouble and that he was lucky that God helped him by showing him the sword. But it was all done, he concludes significantly, so that men might sleep safe in Heorot and so that the community of king and people might be restored to its proper function once again. Grendel, so often called mankind's enemy, has now been destroyed by Beowulf, mankind's friend.

LESSONS OF THE WAR

Although the real action of Part I of the poem (that is, the scenes in Denmark) is essentially over at this point, there is an interlude of some 500 lines before the real action of the second part begins, at line 2200, with the coming of the fire dragon to Beowulf's kingdom fifty years later. During this interlude, Hrothgar makes a long didactic speech, and then, after a little more conversation, Beowulf and his men embark and sail swiftly back to Geatland, where the hero summarizes his adventures in Denmark for the benefit of his uncle, King Hygelac.

Some critics have condemned this slackening of the narrative as inartistic, and some have attributed the defect to a rather clumsy welding together of several originally separate short poems. Examining the evidence for the latter hypothesis is far beyond the scope of this study; it can only be said here that, although traces of repetition and slight inconsistency are detectable and may well suggest such a welding process, it is hardly possible for us now to isolate and recover the original short poems. In any event, it is perforce the welder we are interested in, for he is the man we have been calling the poet up till now. The first part of the poem surely offers us enough proof of his artistic skill to require us to treat him with respect, and we should be slow to condemn his ineptitude before we have made an earnest attempt to understand what his purpose seems to have been in this part of the poem.

Hrothgar's long speech, for example, may seem digressive or unnecessary to some readers, but one can defend its occurrence in terms of the poet's practice elsewhere. Whereas the first fight with Grendel, as we saw, contained much commentary and ethical generalizing by the poet, the fight with Grendel's mother was almost entirely a matter of physical action. We should bear in mind, how- ever, that the style of heroic poetry is persistently sententious and admits no action that cannot be viewed—and is not explicitly viewed—as ethical. On this assumption, Hrothgar's sermon is, one might almost say, the large dose of moralizing that is overdue, a meditation on certain issues implicit in Beowulf's very success. What is achievement and what is strength? How does a man come to have such powers, and how is he to use them wisely? In what kind of universe does he live, and what is likely to happen to him in the course of a lifetime? These seem to be the questions that Hrothgar is pondering.

The text of his sermon is not a set of words so much as it is an object, the hilt of the giant sword that Beowulf has brought back from the mere and placed in his hand. We are told that it was made unimaginably long ago for some owner whose name is still on the hilt, carved in magic runic letters; then it came into the hands of the Grendel race; then Beowulf took it away from them; now the king holds it in his hand and sees inscribed on it the story of the ancient struggle between God and the giants and of their destruction in the Flood (this story is based on details in the sixth and seventh chapters of Genesis). All these changes in ownership, all these violent fluctuations in fortune, and yet within the changes perhaps some pattern of divine order. In such a paradoxical world of both change and stability, how is a man to keep and assert his own identity? If we think of the poem in musical terms, this description of the hilt and its owners already whispers a sad melody that will become the dominant motif of the last third of *Beowulf.*

Yet in the immediate context of the scene the hilt is undeniably a trophy and a symbol of success, and Hrothgar begins his speech by praising the hero who has won such unthinkable victory. Again, as in the Danes' earlier praise of Beowulf by comparing him with Sigemund, the hero must be measured against the ever-present background of the heroic past. Anyone who knows that past well, claims Hrothgar, will be compelled to grant Beowulf's pre-eminence and the certainty of his future fame among men of all nations. "You have upheld all in patience, combining your strength with wisdom of spirit," he continues, drawing attention to that same self-discipline in the hero that we saw earlier in the poem.

By now Hrothgar is obviously thinking of Beowulf's future career and is regarding him (although we have never considered him this way before in the poem) as a potential king: "You are bound to become a comfort to your people for many long years, and a help to men." Again, as in the previous Sigemund episode, Heremod, the antithesis of the good king, is now introduced. Like Beowulf, Heremod had been granted the marvelous gift of strength by mighty God, but he had become savage, refusing to bestow rings on his men and slaughtering the companions of his feasting table, and at last was exiled far from his kingdom, becoming an outlaw like Cain and Grendel.

In the characters of Beowulf and Heremod Hrothgar has dramatized two moral choices; now he drives the same point home by describing the career of a man of high rank who is tempted by prosperity and falls. The story is a little like the exemplum, or illustrative anecdote, of the typical medieval sermon. Bountiful God pours such blessings on this fortunate man—wisdom, land, power —"that he himself in his folly cannot imagine any end to it." But surely one lesson this poem makes plain, if it does nothing else, is that there is always an "end to it" and man must realize and face that fact; there is always an "until" arriving to terminate man's happiness and glory. The man in Hrothgar's exemplum refuses to imitate as he should the divine generosity that gave him so much: "what he has held for so long seems too little to him, and he becomes fiercely covetous, no longer giving rings in his glory." After a Heremodlike career he dies, and a wastrel heir takes over his wealth.

Hrothgar turns now to Beowulf and earnestly pleads with him:

> Oh, guard yourself against that violent evil, dear Beowulf, best of men! Choose the better part, the ways that are eternal; do not be distracted by proud thoughts, glorious hero. The flowering of your strength is only for a little while. In an instant sickness or sword's edge will cut off that strength, or else it will be fire's embrace or the wave's surge, the stab of steel or an arrow's flight, or horrible old age, or the brightness of your eyes will flicker and darken. Very suddenly, O great prince, death will conquer you. (1758–68)

Similar warnings against pride occur in much medieval preaching and the Christian flavor of this passage is unmistakable, but it should be borne in mind that the attitude found here is characteristic of heroic poetry as well. Beyond all other men, the epic hero is the one who commits himself to living unbearably close to death; he must make this commitment deliberately and in the full consciousness of what death is. Nowhere is this point made more unforgettably than in the *Iliad*: when Achilles at last goes out to avenge Patroclus by killing Hector, he goes *knowing* that he is thereby bringing on his own early death. For man, death is the final limit, and the acceptance of limits is the main theme of Hrothgar's sermon. Although heroic poetry typically pictures the greatest possible enlargement and expansion of self out into some measure of control of the external world, it must also recognize and define a limit to the expansion. Without such recognition, it is in danger of becoming fantasy, romance, or superstitious myth.

Hrothgar ends his sermon by offering Beowulf his own experience as one way of making his message even more emphatic and immediate. Hrothgar lived so many joyful years in his kingdom that he too came to believe that he had no enemy under heaven, no limits surrounding him—and then Grendel came, bringing grief after joy. But now it is evident that joy can also follow grief; the king thanks God that he has lived to see Grendel's bloody head before him. The message on the sword hilt has been borne out; there is a divine justice in the violent rhythms of life.

Now it is time for Beowulf to return home. The following morning he takes leave of Hrothgar, thanking him courteously for his hospitality and offering him his help in the event that it should ever be needed again. His speech illustrates well the way the poem is now shifting its focus from the single-handed exploit of the individual to the broader activities of the political world, a movement which of course foreshadows Beowulf's own development from youthful hero into mature king. Now Beowulf tells Hrothgar that he will be able to bring a thousand men to Denmark if Hrothgar should need them, since the hero knows he will be able to count on Hygelac's support of such an expedition. Beowulf seems very conscious of diplomatic realities in this speech. He goes on to invite Hrothgar's son Hrethric to visit the Geatish court, where he will find firm friends. Perhaps he is thinking here of the threat to Hrethric's succession to the throne which Hrothulf represents. At the time of the great banquet, Beowulf merely listened in silence to Wealhtheow's anxious pleas; now we see him taking action on the basis of his understanding of the situation she hinted at.

Hrothgar is positively staggered, it seems, by the revelation of this new dimension of Beowulf's talents. Only God could have put such words in his mouth, he exclaims, for the king has never before heard a young man speak with more mature intelligence. In his enthusiasm Hrothgar predicts that the Geats will have to choose Beowulf as their king some day. Not only has Beowulf restored and revitalized the community of Heorot, he has now established firm ties of peace between the Geats and Danes. At this point we can perceive that the pattern of the poem up to now has been tracing the expansion of the hero's beneficent power outward from himself alone to his little band of followers, then to the Danish hall and the evil mere, and now finally to international peace. Yet it may be that all this glory is shadowed a little in this intensely emotional farewell scene by old Hrothgar's sure intuition that, for all their promises, they will never see each other again. Whatever his insight, only age itself can bring this kind of deep knowledge to young Beowulf.

Imperturbably Beowulf and his men now sail back to the country of the Geats, leaving behind them an old king and returning to a young king, leaving Denmark with its great past and dubious future and returning to a nation whose glory is apparently yet to come. Perhaps the voyage is another way of representing change and the passage of time, specifically of representing the change of role that the hero must now undergo. The new world of political power and responsibility he is entering is also reflected in the digression (beginning about line 1925) which compares the type of the Good Queen, Hygelac's young wife Hygd, with the Bad Queen, Thryth, an evil female of ancient times who cruelly executed any man who dared to look at her. "That is no queenly way for a lady to behave, no matter how good-looking she may be," the poet observes mildly, and he goes on to tell approvingly of how this shrew was tamed when King Offa of the Angles took her in marriage and made a good queen out of her at last.

In response to his uncle Hygelac's eager inquiries, Beowulf must now tell of his adventures in Denmark. That there is some degree of repetition in Beowulf's retelling of the events is the sort of thing that may strike a modern reader as tiresome and inartistic, but the original audiences for epic narrative do not seem to have minded repetition as much as we do, as one can certainly see, for instance, in the verbatim reproduction of messages in the Homeric poems. In any event, the poet of *Beowulf* is remarkably successful in avoiding any real tedium in this retelling. The descriptions of the two fights are quite brief, but they are interesting if for no other reason than that we really are curious to know how Beowulf himself regards these encounters. And much new information is provided in the retelling. Now that he is back home, Beowulf can tell us his impressions of Denmark without the restraints of politeness. He is critical of Hrothgar's judgment in proposing the political marriage of his daughter Freawaru (who was not even mentioned the first time the tale was told) to Ingeld of the Heathobards, and he predicts a new outbreak of the feud between the two tribes. We also

learn for the first time (because this is the kind of thing Hygelac
would particularly want to know) the name of the Geat who
was devoured by Grendel, and Beowulf tells us now of the interesting *glof*, the giant mitten or food bag, that Grendel lugged hope-
fully to Heorot. Because Hygelac is also presumably interested
in what other kings do, Beowulf describes at some length how
Hrothgar himself took the harp and performed at the great banquet
(an incident never mentioned earlier), and how he presented the
Geats with gifts.

In itself Beowulf's long and candid speech to his beloved king
dramatizes a relationship of great importance to the poem. We
see this entire story being offered to Hygelac as a rich gift by his
loyal nephew and subject. Beowulf ends his speech with what is
virtually a formula of presentation:

> And that is how the mighty king [Hrothgar] lived, in accordance with
> the old customs. I did not come out behind in the gifts proffered as a
> reward for my strength, for the son of Healfdene gave me all the
> treasure I could ask for. And now I want to bring these things here,
> O warrior king, and offer them to you with my devotion. All my
> joys now depend on you, for apart from you I have few close kinsmen,
> Hygelac. (2144–51)

In words and gestures like these Beowulf turns fully toward his king,
taking a stance wholly in relationship to him, and we are meant
to feel the emotional depth of this relationship. Perhaps only now
for the first time we realize why Beowulf was first introduced in the
poem as "Hygelac's thane" (line 194) and why he spoke so often of
his king all during his stay in Denmark, as he did, for instance, in
the speech he made before entering the mere.

Now Beowulf formally presents his king with the gifts and royal
heirlooms he has received from Hrothgar. It seems clear that the
poet wants us to view this ceremonial as an epiphany of the ideal
functioning of heroic society, at the climactic moment when the
properly rewarded hero surrenders the tokens of his achievement
to his beloved king, thereby voluntarily subordinating his individual glory to the greater glory of the family-state. The poet is here
significantly sententious:

This is how a kinsman should behave—and not be secretly weaving a treacherous net for others or laying a deathtrap for a comrade. His war-tough nephew was indeed very loyal to Hygelac, and each of them was attentive to the happiness of the other. (2166–71)

And after Beowulf presents the necklace that Wealhtheow had given him to Queen Hygd, the poet comments once more:

In this way Beowulf, a man known in battles, showed his bravery in heroic deeds, and lived to gain glory; never was he the one to strike comrades over drinks by the hearth, never was his temper savage. No, with the greatest strength of mankind this valorous man kept safe the abundant gifts that God had given him. (2177–83)

As both passages show, what a hero is must characteristically be defined in part by what he is not—the merely violent man who wilfully desecrates the bonds of comradeship and kin. The lesson preached by Hrothgar in his sermon is essentially the same lesson here conveyed by Beowulf's actions. The strength God gives a man can always be (and perhaps most often is) diverted toward actions harmful to the human community. What makes the true hero in this poem is not the strength itself but how it is applied to desirable social ends; not the mere ferocity but the ability to control the ferocity and channel it into the form of a personal dedication to one's superiors and inferiors that is both clear-eyed and passionate, tranquil and absolute.

⊷ III ⊷

BEOWULF IN GEATLAND

PROBLEMS OF STRUCTURE

Now, suddenly, in the space of a few lines, we move from the brightly lit scene celebrating the triumphant homecoming of the young Beowulf to the last dark day of the hero's life, some fifty years later. Few literary works make such startling leaps in fictional time, and are so ready to sacrifice opportunities to fill in the events of their hero's career. One can sympathize with the barely suppressed resentment of those commentators who have complained that *Beowulf* deals only with the fringes of things, with first beginnings and final endings, leaving all the rich material at the center of the lives of men and nations almost untouched. And here again some have fallen back on the "badly welded" theory, maintaining that we are merely foolish to insist on regarding as a unified poem what is clearly a small anthology of separate stories about a single heroic figure.

We can only reply to those who deny the essential unity of the poem in the same terms we used earlier. It may well be that modern readers are a little too quick to pursue the sacred chimera of organic unity in the poems they take in hand, but it is hard not to believe that some Anglo-Saxon, whether poet, scribe, or revising editor, put *Beowulf* together the way he did because he saw a rightness and an esthetic beauty in the arrangement. We can see this rightness too, I believe, although the unity of *Beowulf* may be of a rather unusual kind, residing in emotional rhythms and contrasts uniquely characteristic of poetry and not always easy to state plainly in discursive language.

Already, in the last chapter, we were proposing one kind of answer to the charge of discontinuity by examining the way the poet gradually modulates the shift of our interest from the activities of a young hero, not yet burdened with responsibilities, toward the concerns of kingship. Hrothgar's didactic address to Beowulf really deals with the problems of kings rather than those of young warriors, because he knows that Beowulf is qualified to be a king and fully expects that he will one day become one. When the hero returns to his own country, this expectation seems to gain more plausibility, and even the careful depiction of Beowulf as the ideal young retainer hints at the same likelihood, for the role of retainer at the court is in itself a political role—at least he is no longer the freelance monster-killer now—and a good king must first learn how to be a good subject.

At the beginning of Part II we see Beowulf not only as king but as a very old and experienced king, and this too was signalled in Hrothgar's sermon, to the extent that the sermon was an old man's warning against the temptations that assail men old enough to have reached the peaks of political power. At the time he listened to the sermon, such problems were of little concern to Beowulf, but in Part II he finds himself faced with all that ever confronted Hrothgar and more.

Hygelac of the Geats plays an important pivotal role that serves to bind the two halves of the poem together. He is mentioned as often in the second part as in the first. Young Beowulf brings all his honors and rewards proudly back to his beloved king at the end of Part I; and long after Hygelac's death the aged Beowulf looks back to him and remembers him with the same intense affection.

But we are moving in the wrong direction, as the reader may already have guessed, in trying to build a case for the unity of the poem on this kind of gradual linear development, and on similarities and consistencies between the two parts, even though such an approach to the question is what seems natural today. It is not the continuity but the very abruptness of the break at line 2200 that is the really significant fact, and if we go back and proceed again from an acceptance of this fact, we may find the poet's workings in their own way as audacious as those of his hero. For he seems to have made deliberate use of the poetic bond formed by differences, by polarization, by the contrast of opposites, to set up a relationship of parts that is entirely consonant with the dominant rhetorical structure of Old English poetry, as we have noticed on many occasions along the way. It follows from this that Part II must logically be as different and discontinuous from Part I as it can well be. A mass of evidence supports this critical hypothesis.

The foreground action of Part II is quickly summarized. Beowulf eventually inherits the Geatish throne, ruling his nation well until the day a dragon, infuriated at having a cup removed from its hoard of treasure by a runaway slave, attacks the Geats and burns the royal hall. The aged king insists on going alone to fight the dragon, but is in grave danger of perishing in the fight before young Wiglaf comes to help him kill the monster. Beowulf dies of his wounds and is given a magnificent funeral by his people.

Although the plot here outlined is of course the main carrier of meaning, other aspects of Part II claim our attention first. It will be noted that the setting and the type of action in Part II are quite different from those in Part I. As we have seen, Part I gave generous space to the high rituals of civilized life in Heorot: the graceful etiquette surrounding host and guest, the proud celebration of a noble tribal past, and, above all, the long and leisurely conversation among happy feasters. The stage in Part I is almost always crowded, for there are many characters, especially if we include, as we should, the memorable characters who appear in the various tales that are told. Beowulf's victories over Grendel and his mother are presented primarily as actions that guarantee the survival of this social fabric: the hero takes command of the threatened hall and guards it, in the end cleansing it and its immediate surroundings of the invading evil so that ring-giving and feasting can continue. What is made most vivid to us in Part I is precisely that busy, noisy, bright-colored world that Beowulf saves.

The second part of the poem, on the other hand, offers us no councils, no feasts, no public rituals of any kind other than a funeral. Indeed, there is not even a hall in which to hold such ceremonies, for the dragon burns the royal palace to the ground when he first comes out enraged from his barrow. What we have instead is the bleak and lonely setting of a windswept hill near the sea, where the main focus of all the action, an ancient grave-barrow with a curse on it, holds its dragon and its treasure far away in time and space from human society. In this setting Beowulf speaks to his small band of retainers and to Wiglaf, and Wiglaf and the Messenger address the Geats, but much of the time these speeches are hardly conversations so much as they are soliloquies or generalized theme-statements. The familiar life of king and warriors together in the hall is a life remembered and recalled to mind in these speeches rather than anything experienced directly. Against the dark background the isolated figures seem lonely and frail.

The movement toward generalization in Part II can be seen most clearly in the introduction of anonymous speakers who give voice to mankind's most profound and intense feelings, yet with a quality of impersonal objectivity or of distanced song. The poet himself might well be thought of as one of these nameless speakers; he seems to make his presence felt to a greater extent in Part II through his comments on events and their implications. The Last Survivor of the ancient race whose treasure was buried in the dragon mound and the Old Father who must helplessly watch his son being hanged are each created solely to utter a single moving and lyrical speech before they disappear again from the poem. The Geatish Messenger who rides back to tell the assembled Geats of Beowulf's death echoes all these voices in his long and eloquent speech; spokesman of a nation and to a nation, he is in turn omniscient, prophetic, and mournfully elegiac. We will look more closely at all these speeches in a moment, but the general point to be made here is that these speakers are scarcely characters at all and do not in themselves create any sense of a social scene. They are not individualized or developed, they may indeed be (like the Old Father) purely hypothetical, and they have little direct dramatic relation to other characters in the poem. In this respect *Beowulf* shares with Old English elegies like *The Wanderer* and *The Seafarer* a marked tendency to move from the presentation of intense personal experience toward the broadest kind of reflective generalizing.

Considered from a certain point of view, perhaps this type of anonymous speaker is the very antithesis of the epic hero. He is without name because he is rendered unable to achieve a name in the only way heroic poetry will permit a name to be acquired, through physical action. Usually the nameless speaker finds himself in an irremediable situation, where he can do nothing but lament his helplessness and misery. In this particular respect, the contrast between the two parts of the poem is very clear. Beowulf's adventures in Denmark, now seen in perspective, are the very epitome of achievement: a massive problem is first stated and then solved by heroic effort, as thoroughly solved as a problem can be. Heorot is altogether saved from external threat; the mere is altogether cleansed of its evil inhabitants; the resulting gratitude of Hrothgar and the Danes is total. On the other hand, from the moment Part II begins we are made painfully conscious of absolute limitations that the universe puts on human achievement.

Another way to approach what is doubtless the same fundamental contrast is through examining the differences in the way time is represented in the two parts. Part I deals with the present, which is partly to say that it is dominated by strenuous action. It is largely made up of blow-by-blow descriptions of actions together with dramatic speeches. Of the past we hear very little, and that little is there only because it is immediately relevant to the present. We must know of Beowulf's youthful exploits because they are evidence of his present powers. We are told about Scyld because he was the one who first established the great tradition of Danish splendor that is still visible around us in the present. There are a few sinister hints about the future—notably the destructive events connected with Hrothulf and Ingeld—but exactly what will happen is not made explicit or much dwelt on. If Queen Wealhtheow is rightfully apprehensive, Hrothgar and the other Danes are not, and Grendel's mother is a clear and present danger of a kind to blot out any vague and formless anxieties.

On the other hand, fully a third of Part II is given over to describing events in the past. The history of the dragon's treasure is touched on at some length; Beowulf reviews his long life in detail, going back to his earliest memories; the poet is constantly making reference to events in the complicated and long-lasting feud between the Geats and their northern neighbors the Swedes. Indeed the whole technique of Part II is to a large extent what the modern novelist would call flashback. On the final day, the *endedæg*, of a man's life, we stand and look back into the past as the hero himself thinks back over his life at the moment that he is aware of the imminence of death. This kind of retrospection is extended and magnified by other points of view as well as Beowulf's—the sad recollections, for instance, of the Last Survivor or of Wiglaf. If anyone reminisced in this way in Part I, it was only the Nestorlike Hrothgar, but in Part II everyone does.

What is at the core of all these differences between the two parts may be called simply, as Tolkien suggested over thirty years ago, the fundamental contrast between youth and age.[1] We can use these terms to represent the contrast between experience seen face to face, with complete immediacy, and experience seen as something almost apart from the perceiving self, something already as good as lost and already given its final form and meaning, something seen at last as a completed life among other lives, and a part now of whatever those other lives have meant. Or we might describe it as a contrast between life lived subjectively and life examined objectively. But all such feeble categories reduce the meaning of a poem that for its last thousand lines is subtle, delicate, and beautifully moving.

EPIC AND ELEGY

We have already had occasion to use the word elegiac in describing the tone of Part II, using the word in a specific rather than general sense, because those lyrics known as the Old English elegies use similar language and create a similar effect. In *The Wanderer*, for example, a speaker gives expression to his lonely suffering as he voyages, lordless and homeless, through a bleak exile world where memories return only to vanish again:

In his mind it seems that he embraces and kisses his dear lord, and lays hands and head on his knee [in the rite of homage], as he had done in days long gone when he took joy in the gift throne. But then the friendless man awakens again and sees before him the pale waves, and the seabirds dipping and spreading their wings, and sleet and snow falling, mingled with hail. (*Wanderer*, 41–48)

The chill of his loneliness is like the chill of death itself. Later in the poem the same speaker (or possibly, as has recently been proposed, a second speaker more capable of broad generalization) sees in a ruined wall the very image of mutability:

He who in wise thought reflects deeply over this wall and this dark life, who is old and can recall many battles, will speak these words: "Where has the horse gone? Where the young man? Where now is the giver of treasure? Where are the feasting benches? Where are the joys of the hall? Ah, the bright cup! Ah, the mailed warrior! Ah, the king's power! How that time has passed away, darkened under night's cover as if it had never been." (*Wanderer*, 88–96)

The reader will notice here not only the retrospective point of view but also the use of those traditional symbols of the heroic society—ring giver, wine cup, mead benches—that serve to represent the highest values in human life, at least in the secular world. The same images appear in *Beowulf* in the markedly elegiac lament of the Last Survivor, as he entrusts his nation's treasures to the grave in the barrow:

Hold now, earth, what men could hold no longer—the possessions of heroes. Good men got these things from you once; now death and terrible evil have taken away every man of my people who has given up this life. They have seen hall-joy! Now I have no one to lift the sword or polish the plated cup or the precious goblet. That host of men went elsewhere. Bright gold will fall from the iron helmet now; those who should mend the battle mask sleep. And the mail shirt that often endured the bite of iron over the breaking of shields now crumbles after its owner, no more to march out to battle beside the fighting man. No joy of harp, no pleasure of song; no fine hawk swoops through the hall, no swift horse stamps in the courtyard. Evil death has sent many a living race on its way! (2247–66)

What the poet dramatizes here is the ultimate failure of human energy and will, and his effect seems to be gained by his many images of weight, falling, inertia. The cherished communal life sustained so long by love and courage now crumbles to earth as a kingdom dies. The objects that make up the treasure buried by the Last Survivor have found their value in the act of being used, but now no one is left to raise the sword or drink from the cup. If these objects outlive their owners it is only for a short time; they too must die.

In the ensuing lines we are told that the Last Survivor wanders alone until "death's wave" rises to touch his heart. Immediately thereafter the undefended barrow is taken over by the dragon, obedient to the blind drive of its strange nature to seek out "heathen gold" and guard it against ever being recovered by human beings. That the dragon appears here in such close association with the death of the Survivor and his nation is representative of its symbolic role in the poem, for it is connected with death in more than one way. Like all dragons, it chooses to inhabit burial mounds. This habit was apparently accepted by the Anglo-Saxons as a fact. More rationally, archeologists have suggested that the traces of large-scale burning around pagan cremation burials were sometimes explained by the Anglo-Saxons as evidence of dragon fire. The dragon's chief purpose in *Beowulf* seems to be to keep the buried grave treasure out of circulation; it is infuriated when a single cup is stolen from its vast hoard and is ready to destroy the entire countryside in revenge.

From a symbolic point of view, to some extent the dragon takes on the ironic image of an antiking. Like a true king, it protects wealth: the compound *hordweard* "treasure guardian" is applied twice to kings and four times to the dragon in the course of the poem. But we come to recognize that the dragon fits the particular Germanic stereotype of the Stingy King, a pattern of all evil in Germanic poetry, and perhaps in other heroic poetry. Agamemnon in the *Iliad,* for instance, in his lack of true generosity of spirit and his obsession with material wealth, seems at times to have something of the same quality. The *Beowulf* poet places the dragon in contrast with King Beowulf in respect to their attitudes toward wealth. Beowulf is called "treasure giver," "prince of rings," and "protector [significantly not of hoards but] of warriors." Furthermore the long flashback that begins about line 2350 tells us not only of Beowulf's earlier exploits in Denmark but of his avenging of the death of his uncle Hygelac in the raid on the continent, of his conscientious refusal to take the Geatish throne when it is offered to him by Hygelac's widow, and of his final accession to it only after the young Heardred has been killed in a feud. In all this, the poet makes clear that what makes a man a king is not the guarding of some pile of valuables but the giving of one's resources selflessly for the public good. In line 2390 we find the same summary formula used in reference to Scyld at the beginning of the poem: *thæt wæs god cyning*, that was a good king. And after Beowulf has approached the mound where the old and monstrous "guardian" squats over its "gold treasures," the poet, as he introduces Beowulf's long speech, refers to the hero as *goldwine* "gold friend," a king who uses his gold only in loving and generous ways for his followers' benefit. If the reader can recognize this contrast between "dead" and "living" treasure, he may better understand the purpose of the Last Survivor's speech.

The second elegiac passage occurs in Beowulf's speech and takes on part of its meaning from the hero's own situation. As Beowulf himself seems to sense, his coming now to the dragon's mound is his coming to his own grave. An old man now, he must sit and rest as he reaffirms, at the edge of the world of death, the heroic values that have made up his life, a life that is now fully shaped and visible because it is almost complete. As he begins to speak (in line 2425), we can see how deeply rooted those values are in his memories of childhood. We see the birth of his sense of loyalty in terms of the intense personal affection he felt for his grandfather Hrethel when, as a doubtless lonely seven-year-old, Beowulf was sent to the royal court to enter upon his education as a nobleman, in accordance with the usual medieval custom. Hrethel was kind to him and treated him like one of his own sons. The poet goes on to enlarge and intensify our feeling of this strong attachment by telling of the tragic accidental killing of one of Hrethel's sons by another, and by adding, in order to give expression to Hrethel's sorrow, the elegiac "simile" of the Old Father who helplessly grieves for his hanged son.

Distinctly alien to our modern way of understanding, however, is the reason given for Hrethel's suffering: even though his son is dead, he cannot *act,* for he can claim no money payment as compensation for his son's death by accident and he can take no vengeance on the killer. Neither is the Old Father in the simile permitted by Germanic custom to take vengeance, since his son has apparently been executed by royal decree as a criminal. Again we can see that the emphasis heroic poetry puts on action is so great that the most intense suffering it can picture arises from a situation where all avenues of action are closed off. But, even if these concepts seem strange to us, the description of the Old Father has long been regarded as one of the most moving passages in the poem.

> In just this way it is a great grief for an old man to have to go through, to have his boy swinging young on the gallows; then he will make up a chant, some painful song, when his boy hangs for the raven's delight and he, though old and wise, cannot help him at all. Always, each morning, the going away of his son will come back to his mind, and he will not be concerned with living on to see another heir in his fortress, when the one reached the end of his deeds by death's compulsion. Sorrowing, he will look at his son's bedchamber, the deserted wine hall, the windswept resting places robbed of joy. Riders and heroes sleep in the grave; there is no sound of the harp, no merriment there in the courts, as there once was. Then he will go to his bed and sing in his loneliness a lament for the one dead; all of it, fields and buildings, seem too big for him. (2444–62)

We can observe in the course of the passage the concrete world of hanged son and bereaved father becoming widened and transformed into the archetypal elegiac world of the Last Survivor and of the elegiac lyrics: a purely emotional world of piercing loneliness and disorientation, a silent ruined world, laid waste by time and death.

In its function as a part of the hero's speech, the passage reveals not only Beowulf's loving compassion for the suffering of Hrethel but his significant attunement to the mournful elegiac mode of Part II. In Part I, Hrothgar may have spoken in something like this vein from time to time, but Beowulf did not. Only now is he capable of this kind of perception. But it is of the greatest importance to see that Beowulf is also capable of more than tender sympathy, both in the past he is describing and in the future he faces. He goes on immediately to tell of the violent fighting between Geats and Swedes which broke out after Hrethel's death, in the course of which Hygelac becomes king. We plunge deeply into action, in other words, and it soon becomes action in which Beowulf himself is involved as he grows older and becomes Hygelac's chief warrior. He recalls now how he once crushed Hygelac's Frankish slayer in his mighty grasp, and the very naked physicality of the act seems to stress that it *was* an act, that Beowulf was able to act out his grief for his dead king to some degree in the soul-satisfying rite of vengeance. And he remembers how he killed Grendel too by the same primitive method, as he now prepares to carry sword and iron shield against the dragon's fire, for bare hands will not serve in this battle. This is not a fight with Grendel, and Beowulf does not live in the past.

Our summary here makes gracelessly a transition from past into present that the poem makes smoothly and effectively. We are to realize that Beowulf is not reliving past glories in some final outburst of senility; he is rather using his action of the past as the ground for present action. His early love for old Hrethel widens to become his love for the family and the nation; his luminous vision of human sorrow and despair has added maturity to his character without weakening his capacity for action. Over the long years he describes in his speech, many men he has known and loved have died, and he knows he too will die, even if he has succeeded in surviving the catastrophes of heroic history up until this moment. But even if his age and loss of strength are hinted at in his reminiscent speech and perhaps reflected indirectly in the appalling power of the adversary he must now face, what counts is that his will is the same will he possessed when he was young, his dedication is the same, the very language of the formal boast he makes before this battle is the same.

Within the bounds of the emotional world the poem offers us, there is nothing Beowulf is not familiar with: he has recognized and experienced love, suffering, bereavement, exultant action, the élan of youth, and the sadness of old age. If his speech had not made this so plain to us, we would marvel less at the old warrior and at his deliberate movement forward to call the dragon out from his barrow to fight.

BEOWULF'S DEATH

Because a stream of fire issuing from the dragon's mound keeps Beowulf from approaching any closer, he must wait for the dragon to respond to his challenge. Alone and indomitable, he sends his "word" echoing in "under the gray stone," stirring the dragon to instant rage at the very sound of a human voice. We cannot reconstruct the responses of the original audience to the dragon, influenced as they must have been by folk beliefs now lost, and we must guess as best we can at the associations with which the poet surrounds it here. Surely he stresses at this point the wholly alien nature of the dragon, not only in relation to human antagonists but even to such humanoid monsters as Grendel and his mother. Why dragons behave as they do is basically inexplicable; all we can gather here is the fact that their hatred for mankind seems to be innate and ineradicable. We are not told of the dragon's thoughts (if it has any), but we see the terrible phenomenon of its venomous and fiery breath; we see the stone vaulting of its grave-dwelling, a sight which doubtless recalled to the Anglo-Saxons those prominent ruins, Roman and pre-Roman, that filled their island with disturbing emblems of mortality; we see its slow, reptilian coiling and uncoiling as it moves toward Beowulf. There is no need to search for an ingenious symbolic interpretation of the dragon in action, moving toward us: this is the implacable oncoming of annihilation, this is the verge of the abyss.

And against it Beowulf stands his ground. This time, the poet reminds us mournfully, the hero's confident expectations will not be fulfilled. His shield cannot protect him; his sword fails to cut deep enough to wound the dragon. Rhetorically the passage moves into a long sad chant of negatives: Beowulf has lost the use not only of weapons but of his companions, and in his isolation must now endure a *nearo,* a very narrow place, he who once ruled the widest spaces. His retainers have fled for safety to a nearby forest. But because Beowulf stands there now and because he has lived the life he has and has described it to his men just now, "in one of them courage surged up against sorrow" and the young warrior Wiglaf comes forward to help his king. Perhaps it is also because of the overwhelming onrush of darkness that we need here a formal and eloquent restatement of heroic values. By his very stance Beowulf of course restates those values, but we want urgently to know whether the code he holds to is transmissible to others.

Wiglaf is introduced to us here as intricately bound into the web of aristocratic relationships and the obligations they imply: son of Weohstan, kinsman and retainer of Beowulf, possessor of a famous sword his heroic father once took from the Swedish prince Eanmund after slaying him. If the code operated mechanically, these relationships in themselves would be enough to insure that Wiglaf would hurry to his royal kinsman's side; but presumably the Geats who ran away from the fight were just as aristocratic and just as obligated as Wiglaf. Indeed that is the very point Wiglaf makes in his speech to them now: he reminds them of the time in the mead hall when Beowulf presented them with their armor and weapons—present symbols of obligation—in return for their promise to repay him by fighting loyally at his side when need arose. Now is the day, Wiglaf continues, that their king's claim on them falls due, and each retainer must now choose individually whether he will honor that claim. Wiglaf shows the way by making his own choice, knowing that it may very well be a choice of death: "For me, God knows that I would much rather have the flame embrace my body along with my gold giver!" Entering the fight, Wiglaf reminds Beowulf of his own youthful vows long ago not to let his glory droop and slacken while he lived, and offers him his help in the fight.

In a way it may seem as though Beowulf's own past, his own youth, takes form and joins him here in the person of Wiglaf, but Wiglaf has more to do with the future than with the past. He represents continuity in time, for by his own free act in response to Beowulf's danger he takes on the great heritage of human responsibility. At this present moment, that responsibility is expressed in the form of collaboration, as the two men take their stand to meet a second onslaught from the dragon. When Wiglaf's wooden shield is consumed by fire, he must take shelter behind his king's shield. As he does this, Beowulf, perhaps in an attempt to cover his retreat, strikes another blow at the dragon, this time delivered so powerfully that his great sword Nægling is shattered. Immediately the dragon makes its third rush and its sharp poisoned teeth close around Beowulf's neck.

"Then," cries the poet triumphantly, "I heard that in the time of need the warrior who stood beside the mighty king made his courage known, and his strength and his bravery, as it was a part of him from birth!" Wiglaf, his hand burned by the fire, moves forward to stab the dragon in a vital spot "a little farther down." And the wounded Beowulf recovers himself enough to use his dagger to cut through the dragon's body. "They killed the enemy, both those noble kinsmen destroyed him," exults the poet, using the plural very pointedly. For it is the loving and self-sacrificing relationship between the two men that itself seems to gain the final victory over the monster, and the ensuing lines which tell of the last moments of Beowulf's life continue to lay great stress on the intimate bond connecting this society of two. Wiglaf laves the wounded Beowulf with water, and then hurries to bring the treasures from the barrow so that Beowulf may look at them before he dies. As he looks at the great strength of the well-built "eternal earth house," Beowulf is thinking of death, and he regrets that he has no son of his own to leave the dragon hoard to, but then he bequeaths the treasure together with the responsibility for the kingdom to Wiglaf. Just as Beowulf himself once became the adopted son of old Hrothgar for a time, now Wiglaf seems to have earned by his courage and devotion something like the title of son to Beowulf. The dying king's last gesture is both ritualistic and intimate: he gives his gold neck ring and his weapons to the young warrior, and "told him to use them well." And his last words are addressed to Wiglaf: "You are the last survivor of our race, the Wægmundings. *Wyrd* [fate] has swept away all my kinsmen to their destiny, warriors in their courage; I must now follow them." (2813–16).

The theme of the transmittal of value down through time, from generation to generation, is in large part focused here, as elsewhere in Part II, on the treasure. If we do not see the hoard as having this intense if sometimes puzzling symbolic significance, it will seem strange to us that during the last few minutes of the hero's life both he and the poet are so absorbed in contemplating the wealth of the hoard. Beowulf, after affirming in eloquent understatement the accomplishments of his long life—I guarded this people for fifty years, not seeking quarrels and not swearing many unjust oaths, and God will have no occasion to blame me for the slaughter of kinsmen when I leave this life—orders Wiglaf to bring treasure out from the dragon hoard for him to examine. His dying will be easier if he knows he is leaving such wealth behind him. We would be in no difficulty if this were all that was said of the treasure, but we also are led to see it from quite different points of view.

Wiglaf now enters the dragon's barrow, and the poet describes the treasure at some length:

> Exulting in victory, the brave kinsman-thane walked away from the seat to where he could see many a precious jewel, gold glittering along the ground, marvels on the wall; he saw the den of the dragon, that old dawn flier, and how cups stood in it, vessels of the men of old, now with no one to polish them and their ornaments all crumbled away. And there was many an ancient rusty helmet there and many an arm ring, fashioned cunningly. Treasure, gold in the ground, can easily overcome [outlast?] anyone of mankind, hide it who will. And he also saw a royal standard of pure gold looming high over the hoard, greatest of all the creations of men's skillful hands; a light blazed out from it so that he could see his way along the floor and run his eyes over the treasures. (2756-71)

The images of unpolished cups and rusty helmets, with their echoes of the Last Survivor's elegiac speech, tell us of the full vanity of human wishes from the perspective of devouring time. But the *segn* of imperishable gold that towers over these mouldering objects, the king's standard, seems to imply just as strongly some kind of survival in the midst of decay. Survival of the ideal of kingship? We recall that a similar golden *segn* was raised over the head of

the dead Scyld as he lay ready to go out to sea in his funeral ship.
Wiglaf takes care to include the great *segn* among the objects he
brings out to show Beowulf.

In some way hard to define—to be too dogmatic about what the
symbol of treasure stands for in *Beowulf* is to be dishonest—the
gold hoard seems to reflect the very ambivalence that men find in
their world. The moralizing remark that the poet makes in the
middle of the passage quoted just now is not indisputably clear
because of one unfamiliar word, but it seems to be a warning about
the malignant powers of gold, possibly here its capacity to reveal
itself or betray its presence no matter how well it has been hidden.
Moreover, later in the poem we are told that the ancients had cast
a mighty spell about the treasure so that no man could ever touch
it until the Day of Judgment; this apparently heathen reference
to magic is quickly followed by the Christian statement that God
(not being affected by such spells) can of course open the hoard
to anyone he selects. Beowulf himself seems to have been granted
God's permission to break into the hoard (though the text here
is again very difficult to be certain about), but even so it may well
have been hard for the audience not to see his death in the process
of getting at the hoard as somehow reflecting the effect of the
curse. We are really left in considerable confusion on the subject
of the treasure, although it may well be that the original audience
understood the poet's view of it well enough. We can only draw the
lame, provisional conclusion that the treasure seems to be incon-
sistently regarded as good and bad, blessed and cursed, with strong
potentialities for both creation and destruction.

Beowulf certainly welcomes the sight of the treasure when Wiglaf
returns from the barrow, and explicitly thanks God that he has
been permitted to leave such wealth for his people. Some have
tried to connect his eagerness for the treasure with the very common medieval theme of the deadly sin of avarice or cupidity,
but Beowulf here surely appears to be generous rather than
avaricious. He believes he can now leave something to his people;
he has made his death worth something tangible. In this context,
as in several other places in the poem, the dragon treasure in all
its immensity seems to become something like a gigantic wergild,

the value of a man's life in Anglo-Saxon law, a material way of setting some price on the worth of Beowulf's life and sacrificial death. That Beowulf's own people come to regard the treasure as having this meaning seems to be implied later in the ritual of the funeral, as we shall see in a moment.

A good name is better than gold in epic poetry, however, and the epic hero's central concern for perpetuating his name is evident in Beowulf's last command to Wiglaf:

> Tell my famous warriors to make a bright mound after my burning, on that high land by the sea. It will tower high on Whale Cliff as a reminder to my people, so high that seafarers in later years will name it Beowulf's barrow, those men who drive their tall ships from far off over the sea's darkness. (2802–8)

The bright barrow of his memory will gleam over the ocean mists like the golden *segn* among the rusting artifacts of the hoard. What Beowulf leaves to his people, in the end, will not be a great accumulation of material wealth but a lived-out example of total devotion, a kind of ethical brightness that will continue to provide an orientation for those sailors and givers of names in the perilous seas of the future.

When Beowulf dies, the poet tells us, in unmistakably Christian terms, that "his soul went out of his breast to go seek the judgment and glory of the just" (2819–20). If we were reading an Anglo-Saxon poem about the life of a saint, we would find that a statement like this would usually be the starting point for an elaborate final development of the theme of the triumphant journey homeward into the joy and security of the other world (Christian poets were not averse to representing it as a return from exile into the Great Mead Hall of God's heroes). But in *Beowulf* this brief remark is almost all we have to suggest the existence of an afterlife as Christians know it. Instead of enlarging on this subject at this point, the poet adds a rather curious meditation on the tableau now formed by the lifeless bodies of Beowulf and the dragon, lying side by side. He lays special stress on the dragon's motionlessness: it lies still now on the earth, where once it used to range exuberantly in playful flights at midnight. In part this passage

belongs to the traditional pattern in heroic poetry of the triumph
over a fallen enemy, but the more the dragon is dwelt on, the
more conscious we become of Beowulf's own immobility. The des-
perate Wiglaf continues to try to revive his king with water, but
this repeated action has no other effect than to remind us that
Wiglaf cannot make his king move again. In the intensely physical
world of epic poetry, death is, above all else, to be strengthless and
inert.

Two Messages

As Wiglaf is in the act of ministering to his dead lord, the
cowardly retainers who ran off into the safety of the forest to
save their lives when the dragon appeared from his barrow now
come slowly back to stare in silence at Wiglaf. At first he seems too
intent on his own grief even to notice them, but finally he raises
his head to give them a "grim answer," a rebuke that takes on
truly heroic proportions.

If the truth were to be told, he says bitterly, Beowulf as good as
threw away all the valuable war gear they are now wearing, for
when the time of need came they were not ready to repay him with
their service. Too few defenders thronged around their lord! So
shocking a collapse of the heroic system will have drastic effects:
all giving and taking of treasure, all relationships between men,
all ownership of property will now come to a stop, once foreigners
learn of their inglorious flight. They have disgraced the nation
(and we are to assume that an unheroic reputation can spread
just as widely and last just as long as a heroic one). Death, Wiglaf
concludes, will be better for every man than a life of such humilia-
tion.

The vehemence of Wiglaf's rebuke has led some readers to see
it as an important final statement, almost as the "moral" of the
poem. It is true that, if we wish to take this band of retainers as
representative of the Geatish nation as a whole (and perhaps
Wiglaf seems to see them in that light), we may be strongly
tempted to draw the conclusion that the Geats' own degenerate
cowardice will be the immediate cause of all the calamities that lie
ahead for them in the near future. But one major difficulty in this

is the fact that these retainers now vanish utterly from the poem, and we move instead to a larger group of Geats who have been waiting for news of the battle out of sight "up over the cliff." These Geats become audience and actors for the remainder of the poem, and the harsh note of Wiglaf's condemnation is never directed at them.

If the apparent inconsistency is troublesome to modern readers, they should realize that Wiglaf's speech of rebuke gains the kind of brief and short-term effect the poet wants, and that inconsistency of this kind is often to be found in poetry close to oral tradition, where the poet is accustomed to working within the limits of the attention span of a listening audience. In such poetry, a poet must focus all his resources on one thing at a time. Here we have been intent on a traditional and significant image, the body of the dead king, and the response of the Germanic mind to such an image has already been shaped and is predictable. In the Old English poem on the battle of Maldon, the surviving members of Earl Byrhtnoth's comitatus make formal vows to avenge their lord's death, and these assertions and calls to action are often constructed on the base of a phrase like "here our lord lies dead on the ground," because a sight like this must itself lead to profound emotion and violent action. In the scene in *Beowulf,* we see two responses: one by Wiglaf, the retainer loyal to the end, and the other by those who had not the strength to remain loyal. The tableau has the same kind of symmetry we see in the two bodies of the king and dragon lying side by side. We need the cowards to set the brave man in even stronger relief, and Wiglaf's searing criticism of their failure balances his earlier appeal to their sense of duty. If the symbolic construction of the scene has achieved the effect designed by the poet, we can in a sense leave it behind us when we move on to another scene built of a different combination of materials.

It is worth adding, however, that such a coldly formal way of analyzing the scene in rhetorical terms does not exhaust its meaning. Surely there is a timeless psychological truth in the very fact that Wiglaf's frantic grief for the king he loved finds expression first in a burst of white-hot rage. Americans of the nineteen-sixties will recognize all too well a similar response in themselves and their neighbors, for we too have suffered the violence of the death of kings. Shock demands an object of rage and blame, and often an emotional prophecy of the imminent collapse of the guilty society.

Wiglaf now asks one of the Geats, the Messenger, to announce the news of Beowulf's death to the main body of Geats who are waiting elsewhere. Like Wiglaf's rebuke of the retainers, the Messenger's long speech is also a prophecy of disaster, but it is pitched in a different key, with its emphasis on the nation rather than the individual. The Messenger is not concerned with fixing responsibility for the death of Beowulf but with revealing to the Geats the future doom now darkening over them as the result of their king's death.

The speech delivered by the Messenger may well be the most effective and important single speech in the poem. It has reminded more than one reader of the often climactic reports of messengers in the ancient Greek tragedies, or, perhaps even more appropriately, of the utterances of the chorus in those plays. There seem to be distinct advantages in having such theme-statements made by speakers who are to a limited extent participants or citizens of the fictional world, but who are much less deeply involved than the main characters and thus capable of greater objectivity. Here one might contrast the personal vehemence of young Wiglaf with the broader historical perspective of the Messenger.

Before the Messenger begins to speak, a scene is set. We are told that the Geatish host has been sitting motionless all the long morning, waiting anxiously for the outcome of the fight. The same familiar image of immobility is carried on into the first lines of the speech, in which the Messenger sketches out a clearly visualized tableau of Beowulf fast in his deathbed, the dragon lying beside him, and Wiglaf sitting and keeping a silent "head watch" over the two bodies. Those accustomed to Old English poetry will be conscious of the potential instability of this kind of arrested action: something is about to explode. What explodes here is the future—what the tableau of the lifeless king necessarily implies and causes: the sudden collapse of that wall of security Beowulf has represented for so long.

In its early stages, the explosion of the future is delayed and controlled. "Now the people have to expect a time of conflict, as soon as the king's fall becomes known to the Franks and Frisians" (2910–13). The Messenger then goes on to explain why these southern tribes feel such hostility toward the Geats as a result of the famous raid that Hygelac once made on their territories. Then the Messenger says that he expects no peace with the Swedes to the north, for they too have long been involved in bitter feuding with Beowulf's people. His tone is that of the political analyst, relatively abstract and general in its way of describing national sentiments. But now, and suddenly, the explosion into vivid and concrete action finds its full release as the swift-moving narrative of the battle of Ravenswood bursts upon us without warning. We remain for many lines in the midst of dramatic and suspenseful action, even though this battle took place far back in the past, almost as far back as the epic imagination can stretch, when the now aged Beowulf was still a child.

The battle of Ravenswood moves us in two temporal directions at once: backward into the past so that we may catch sight of the deep roots, the very quality of fatedness, of this ancient hatred between two neighboring peoples; and forward into a certain future of anarchy and violence that will crash in on the long-peaceful Geats with the same suddenness that the account of the battle falls clamorously on our consciousness here. But it is able to move in those directions only because it is successful in re-creating in us above all the felt sense of lived-through action in the present. In creating this sense, the passage is unique in the poem. Wars and feuds have been constantly alluded to and hinted at throughout Part II, but these references have been only thunder muttering on a far horizon. Now we are in the storm.

It is a swirl and drumming rhythm of ferocity, dread, and triumph. The Swedish king Ongentheow, "old and terrible," attacks the invading Geats in order to rescue his wife whom they have captured in the raid, and succeeds in killing Hæthcyn, the Geatish king, in the course of the attack. The sentence will not let us pause for breath: Ongentheow's outraged and vengeful impetus drives the lordless Geats ahead of it into Ravenswood, where they huddle through a long miserable night, listening to the furious old king threatening to slaughter and hang them in the morning (possibly, as has recently been suggested, an echo of the pagan Germanic custom of sacrificing battle victims to the war god Odin, or Woden). We feel Ongentheow's rage because it is clearly motivated and understandable, taking indeed the form of righteous indignation.

But, significantly, the account of Ravenswood takes no sides. We feel just as keenly the terror of the Geats, and their immense relief when morning brings not mass hangings but the welcome sound of the trumpets of Hygelac as he comes to their rescue with another detachment of Geatish troops. The exciting seesaw action of the battle is kept moving without pause as Ongentheow, now apparently outmatched, retreats to a more defensible position behind an earthwork. Here he is at last brought to bay (and this hunting term is used in the Old English) by the onrushing Geats. Now the camera abandons its sweeping panoramic shots of mass action for a closer focus on a hand-to-hand fight between Ongentheow and two young Danish warriors, Wulf and Eofor. The incidental fact that their names mean "wolf" and "boar" seems worthy of attention, if taken together with the unremitting savagery of the battle and the name of the forest in which it takes place. The battle of Ravenswood is thereby generalized so that it becomes an archetype of Battle, almost verging on allegory.

The dauntless fight of an old man against two young men in itself has an archetypal flavor. Indeed we find the same fight, or one suspiciously like it, in a story told by the Danish chronicler Saxo Grammaticus about 1200, although it involves three other characters from Scandinavian heroic legend. Saxo's tale makes it very plain that the audience's sympathy is with the old man in a fight like this, and that the two young warriors gain little real glory by their victory. Even though the version in *Beowulf* is more objectively told, the audience is surely expected to respond with admiration to the old king's last stand rather than to think of him as one of the enemy from the Geatish point of view. On the other hand, there is no sentimental lingering over the Swedish king's death. After killing him, Eofor methodically strips him of his armor and weapons and carries them to his lord Hygelac, who expresses his gratitude to the two brothers by granting them great rewards.

Even though heroic decorum is thus observed by Hygelac, we may feel the same kind of irony here that we felt at the end of the Finn story in Part I, where we watched the Danes plundering Finn's hall and carrying his widow triumphantly back to Denmark. In both cases a context of loss and disaster makes the traditional ceremonies of triumph ring hollowly. The very success of the Geats in this battle, the gallantry of Wulf and Eofor, the munificence of the royal rescuer Hygelac, all are qualified and sapped in more than one way. We saw that the victory over old Ongentheow is a little flawed, and in any case we can be sure that the political effect of the king's death—because it is so unforgettable—will be to increase Swedish hostility toward the Geats, and to increase it in direct proportion to the degree of gloating indulged in by the Geats.

Still, so long as the pressure of the narrative continues, we are granted little time to reflect on such matters, and in this respect we are like the participants themselves. If we are conscious of anything in particular at the conclusion of the account of the battle, it is of the justice of celebrating Hygelac's generosity. Only when, in line 2999, the Messenger himself begins to comment on the larger implications of his story are we aware that we have been fully immersed in such a vivid present that we have almost forgotten how long ago all that took place, how long ago the generous Hygelac himself died, and how the Geats can expect no more rescues like that one in the future.

The Messenger makes explicit the didactic purpose of his exemplary tale:

> *That* is the violence and hostility, murderous clash of men, that I expect to see when the Swedish people invade us, after they have learned that our lord is dead. (2999–3003)

Now we recognize that our chief impression of Ravenswood is of participation in violence, as we are abruptly moved back out of the short-range heroic moment, the framed scene with the moving figures of named characters, to the wider world of political implication, and out of the past seen as present to us toward the past seen as future, a threat both immediate and of infinite duration. The Messenger goes on to predict warfare, enslavement, and misery for his nation, but his prophecy would have little of the poetic force it has if the fight at Ravenswood had not been brought so close to us, if we had not been compelled to run the tumultuous course of its exultant and appalling sensations.

Suddenly we recognize that one most important function of the tale of Ravenswood has been to set a great value on the hero of the poem, for we glimpse the true heroic hell at Ravenswood, a heart of darkness, and we know now that only Beowulf was able to interpose himself to save his people from that hell, as he once went out to exorcize the other kind of hell that threatened Hrothgar's Denmark. Even though in the account of the battle it was Hygelac who took on that symbolic role, it is really Beowulf and not Hygelac who is the saviour-king.

Exactly how the Messenger makes his transition from political history to the full-throated elegiac tone of his conclusion may puzzle our sense of logic but not our sense of poetic rightness. After referring to Beowulf's long defense of his people, he suggests appropriate actions for himself and his listeners: to look at their great king and to carry his body to the funeral pyre. Treasure is apparently to be placed on this pyre to "melt with the brave one," that immense treasure purchased by Beowulf's life. But as the flames devour and obliterate the precious objects, they seem to transform themselves into the flames of future destruction and future war, for now we see images of a warrior with no heirloom to carry, or of a beautiful girl walking wretchedly as a slave in some foreign land. Treasure has been relinquished, and with it the world of the harp, the world of peace, for now there will only be the spear, "morning-cold," lifted again and again for battle, and the harsh cries of ravens and eagles over a battlefield that seems to stretch on forever. The familiar language of the passage, an elegiac style used elsewhere in laments for the far past, gives us the strange sense that this predicted future is already in the past, or that perhaps it is not in time at all, or in some dark time when only ravens will be heard over the ruins of man's achievement, and the ultimate Ravenswood will come into being. If the conventional beasts of battle come to seem half-human here—we see the raven chatting with the eagle about his rivalry with the wolf over the carrion—the battle the Messenger described showed us human beings behaving with bestial ferocity. And now croaks and howls blot out the harp's sound.

In his *Preface to Paradise Lost,* C. S. Lewis cites this passage from *Beowulf* in support of the following observations on the world of epic poetry:

> Much has been talked of the melancholy of Virgil; but an inch beneath the bright surface of Homer we find not melancholy but despair. "Hell" was the word Goethe used of it. It is all the more terrible because the poet takes it all for granted, makes no complaint. . . . Beowulf strikes the same note. Once the king is dead, we know what is in store for us: that little island of happiness, like many another before it and many another in the years to follow, is submerged, and the great tide of the Heroic Age rolls over it.[2]

But he goes on to make a distinction between Homer and *Beowulf.*

> *Beowulf* is a little different. In Homer the background of accepted, matter-of-fact despair is, after all, a background. In *Beowulf* that fundamental darkness comes out into the foreground and is partly embodied in the monsters. And against those monsters the hero fights. No one in Homer had fought against the darkness.

A FUNERAL

Beowulf had fought against the darkness. The concluding 150 lines of the poem are a meditation on that fact and the acting out of a communal response to it. The very fact is above all marvelous, what the Anglo-Saxons called a *wundor.* The weeping Geats now make their way to a point where they can look at the strange scene described at the beginning of the Messenger's speech: their beloved ring giver stretched out in death; the incredible dragon, fifty feet in length; the ambivalent treasure, infinitely precious and "eaten through," "gold of the ancients, wound about with a spell," and now revealed to men only by God's intervention. The scene is something for them to "read," as the symbol-making medieval mind tended to read whatever it saw, and its meaning is plain and final, yet wonder still dominates the reactions of the Geats and of the poet, for we are looking at what man can never take into full comprehension.

> It is a mystery (*wundor*) just when it will be that a courageous man makes the journey to the end of the life decreed him, when he can no longer go on living in the mead hall with his kinsmen. (3062–65)

Wiglaf now speaks once more, not this time setting himself apart from the Geats and condemning them, but merging his own experience with the common experience of the mourning nation. The sense of "we," of community and relationship, is very strong in this speech. We were not able, Wiglaf tells them, to hold Beowulf back from attacking the dragon; he held to his high destiny. When I brought treasure out of the hoard for him to see, he told me to greet you all and asked that you build him a high barrow. Wiglaf then invites the Geats to share his experience in examining the hoard while the pyre is being made ready, and then to "carry our lord, the beloved man, to where he shall long dwell in the Ruler's protection." Under Wiglaf's direction, the Geats now move in cooperative ritual acts: gathering wood for the pyre, collecting treasure from the hoard and loading it on a wagon which also serves as Beowulf's bier, and disposing of the dragon's gross hulk by pushing it over the cliff into the sea.

It will be noticed that the images that seem to predominate in this section, as indeed through much of Part II, are images of weight, of heavy bodies and objects lying still and requiring great effort in the lifting and transporting. It is hard not to associate these images very directly with the physical feel of grief, the weary heft of sorrow. All must be painfully lifted and carried; the laboring wagon transports both the immense treasure and the body of Beowulf to the pyre on Whale Cliff, and the weight is dead weight. We saw earlier in the Last Survivor's speech how the concept of "dead" and inert treasure was developed. Insofar as this hoard is no longer of real use to any living man, it is quite dead now. With Beowulf gone, the Geats seem to be following the suggestion of the Messenger by renouncing the hoard by placing it back in the grave-barrow, "gold in the ground, where it now still lives as useless to men as it was before" (3167–68). Yet paradoxically it may be felt that the very employment of the treasure as a part of the funeral ceremony is a legitimate "use" of it, perhaps the only possible use.

One can think of this funeral as a ring of half-nameless Geats around a name, around a center of meaning which they are at the same time acknowledging and building through their own solemn actions as they carry out their ceremonial movements. They hang the pyre with helmets, shields, and mail shirts—trophies and memories—and place the king's body in the middle. Then they kindle a great fire that burns on, its roaring flames mingled with their weeping, until the body is consumed. Smoke and flame rise high together with the "sorrow song" of an unnamed Geatish woman (the text is unluckily defective at this crucial point in the manuscript) who foresees hardship and slavery for herself. Both flame and song seem to be offerings of some kind to the Unknown. The phrase "heaven swallowed the smoke" might be taken as indicating supernatural acknowledgment of the rite, but if so it is a cryptic answer, and the phrase may simply mean that the smoke plume rose to the great height befitting a great man's burning.

The towering column of smoke and flame is part of a counterpattern of images of rising and of height that is carried further as the Geats build a great mound over the ashes of the pyre, a mound high and broad, visible from a great way off, and then encircle it with a well-made wall, and place in it the mighty dragon hoard. Then twelve Geatish horsemen begin to ride around the barrow, their eyes and thoughts turned inward toward the great center of the poem, their mouths singing the praises of their king. Such a ceremonial ride was apparently an ancient pagan tradition, for the Gothic historian Jordanes tells of singing horesmen riding around the body of King Attila of the Huns. Here the Geats' riding is the climax of the poem's long restatement of the heroic code, for these men ride in the full majesty of the bitter knowledge of their own imminent doom as a nation, acting still "as it is proper to do" in voicing their praise and love for their king. They imitate the same warm and unwavering attitude of respect that Beowulf had always shown toward his beloved Hygelac, and at the end they grant him what the last word of the poem tells us he was most eager to have—

lof, praise, that fame of the hero that lives beyond the burning and the darkness.

A hero is a man, and somehow more than a man. Wiglaf and the grieving Geats see Beowulf as a man known and loved well by them; the Messenger sees him as a tangible felt presence in the solid world of history; when Beowulf reminisces about his life, we feel we know him better than we have known him before in the poem. The poet never lets go of this real and personal dimension to the very end. Yet a mysterious and half-mythic atmosphere surrounds the funeral rites, perhaps largely because we half-recognize the striking of those same notes of feeling we heard in the description of Scyld's funeral at the beginning of the poem. Scyld was assuredly something more than a man, and his career was the purest myth—drifting as a child over the sea to Denmark, saving the Danish nation, and then drifting in his funeral boat back to wherever it was he came from. The similarity does not imply that Beowulf is a god, but it lays stress on the hero's role as rescuer, protector, shield of his people, on the sheer wonder of his existence and his death, and hints at some possible unknown order beyond the known seas of men.

But it is better that Beowulf not be a myth or a god. In reciting their elegy the Geatish riders "speak about a man." One would have thought that the poet could not have matched the intense beauty of the Scyld prologue, but he does so in the funeral of Beowulf. The great barrow around which the Geats ride is the poem itself, and the man himself, a brave and gentle man and known to us.

✑ APPENDIX I ✑

CHRONOLOGY

98 A.D. First description of Germanic society in Tacitus' *Germania*.

c. 410 Withdrawal of Roman troops from the Roman province of Britain.

c. 450–600 Invasion of Britain by numerous bands of Germanic tribesmen (Angles, Saxons, Jutes, Frisians, et al.); warfare with the native British or Welsh.

c. 521 Date of raid by Hygelac on the continent (an event mentioned in *Beowulf*), recorded by the Frankish historian Gregory of Tours.

597 Augustine, sent by Pope Gregory the Great, arrives at Canterbury to undertake conversion of Anglo-Saxons to Christianity.

650–660 Royal ship burial at Sutton Hoo in East Anglia.

663 Synod of Whitby, resolving dispute between Celtic and Roman Christians.

Before 680 Cædmon, monk of Whitby, divinely inspired to compose Christian poetry in English, according to Bede.

c. 671–735 Life of Bede, Northumbrian scholar and author of the "Ecclesiastical History of the English People."

700–750 Most generally accepted date for the composition of *Beowulf*.

735–804 Alcuin of York, who became teacher at the court of Charlemagne.

793 Sacking of the monastery at Lindisfarne by Vikings initiates many decades of raiding and invasions.

849–899 King Alfred the Great of Wessex (ruled 871–899), who stops Viking onslaughts and initiates cultural reconstruction of England.

937   The battle of Brunanburh, a victory over invaders from the north; subject of a poem.

991   The battle of Maldon, an English defeat in a new series of Viking attacks; subject of a poem.

c. 1000   Probable date of the manuscript, Cotton Vitellius A. XV, in which the poem *Beowulf* is included.

1066   Victory of the Norman-French at Hastings; end of the Anglo-Saxon period.

1571–1631 Sir Robert Cotton, early owner of the *Beowulf* MS.

1705   Humphrey Wanley publishes a brief catalogue account of the opening lines of *Beowulf*.

1731   *Beowulf* MS survives destruction by fire.

1815   Thorkelin, an Icelander, first publishes *Beowulf*.

1939   Excavation of the Sutton Hoo mound.

⋖§ APPENDIX II §⋗

FURTHER READING

Historical Background: Standard histories of the period are those of F. M. Stenton, *Anglo-Saxon England* (2d ed., 1947), and R. H. Hodgkin, *A History of the Anglo-Saxons* (2 vols., 3d ed., 1952). Two interesting general studies in paperbound form are by Peter Hunter Blair: *An Introduction to Anglo-Saxon England* (1959) and *Roman Britain and Early England,* 55 B.C.–A.D. 871 (1963 and 1966), the first volume in the Norton Library History of England. Also readily available is the second volume in the Pelican History of England by Dorothy Whitelock, *The Beginnings of English Society* (1952). Also by Dorothy Whitelock is the interesting short study, *The Audience of Beowulf* (1951). Charles Green, *Sutton Hoo: The Excavation of a Royal Ship-Burial* (1963) is an abundantly illustrated description of the famous archeological discovery. Students who like maps will find engrossing the historical *Map of Britain in the Dark Ages,* published by the British Ordnance Survey (2d ed., 1966).

Literary History: There is no need to single out here the various accounts of the period included in the standard literary histories. Stanley B. Greenfield, *A Critical History of Old English Literature* (New York, 1965) is recommended as being concise, well-documented and up-to-date; it is available in paperbound form. Selections of translations of Old English poetry other than *Beowulf* include R. K. Gordon, *Anglo-Saxon Poetry* (2d ed., 1954), in prose; Charles W. Kennedy, *An Anthology of Old English Poetry* (1960), in verse; and Burton Raffel, *Poems from the Old English* (2d ed., 1964), in verse, some of them very successful.

Beowulf: The most-used scholarly text of the original poem is that of Fr. Klaeber, *Beowulf and the Fight at Finnsburg* (3d ed., 1950), which contains an information-packed introduction and copious notes. R. W. Chambers, *Beowulf: An Introduction* (3d ed., with a supplement by C. L. Wrenn, 1959) is a highly readable treasury of information and speculation, largely on the sources and analogues, many of which it reproduces with translations. Most of the recent criticism exists in the form of journal articles, some of which are collected in *An Anthology of Beowulf Criticism,* ed. Lewis E. Nicholson (1963), an array of uneven quality, and in *The Beowulf Poet,* a volume in the Twentieth Century Views series, ed. Donald K. Fry (1968). Book-length studies include Arthur G. Brodeur, *The Art of Beowulf* (1959), and Edward B. Irving, Jr., *A Reading of Beowulf* (1968), the latter containing an up-to-date bibliography of recent critical articles.

Heroic Poetry: C. M. Bowra, *Heroic Poetry* (1952; reprinted 1961) is an encyclopedic survey of heroic poems from many different cultures; the same approach on a smaller scale can be found in Jan de Vries, *Heroic Song and Heroic Legend,* trans. B. J. Timmer (1963). The oral-formulaic hypothesis is stated in Albert B. Lord, *The Singer of Tales* (1964). On the genre of epic generally, the first chapter of Thomas Greene, *The Descent from Heaven: A Study in Epic Continuity* (1963), is extremely useful.

PRONUNCIATION GUIDE

This is a very rough guide to pronunciation of the most common names:

Beowulf (BAY-oh-wulf)
Breca (BRECK-uh)
Ecgtheow (EDGE-thay-oh)
Freawaru (FRAY-uh-wah-ruh)
Grendel (GREN-del)
Hengest (HEN-jest)
Heorot (HEH-uh-rot)
Heremod (HERR-uh-moad)
Hildeburh (HILL-duh-boorg)
Hrethel (HRAY-thuhl)
Hrothgar (HROATH-gahr)
Hygelac (HEE-yeh-lahk)
Ongentheow (ON-yen-thay-oh)
Scyld (SHILD)
Unferth (OON-fayrth)
Wealhtheow (WELK-thay-oh)
Wiglaf (WEE-lahf)

The name of Beowulf's people in southern Sweden, the *Géatas* or Geats, seems to have no single accepted modern pronunciation. If the name had come down into Modern English it might now be YEETS; but it may be most prudent to imitate the Old English pronunciation and call them YAY-ahts.

✎ NOTES ✎

Chapter I

1 Nora K. Chadwick, "The Monsters and Beowulf," *The Anglo-Saxons: Studies Presented to Bruce Dickins*, ed. Peter Clemoes (1959), pp. 171–203.

2 *Historia Ecclesiastica*, Book II, Chap. XII; trans. Dorothy Whitelock, *English Historical Documents*, I [c. 500–1042] (1955), 617.

3 The Latin original of the passage is quoted in a note to p. xxxv of Klaeber's edition of *Beowulf*.

4 The entry under 755 [correctly, 757] in the Parker Chronicle, trans. G. N. Garmonsway, *The Anglo-Saxon Chronicle* (rev. ed., 1954), p. 48.

5 *English Historical Documents*, I, 730–31.

6 See Sune Lindqvist, "Sutton Hoo and *Beowulf*," *Antiquity*, XXII (1948), 131–41, and Charles Green, *Sutton Hoo: The Excavation of a Royal Ship-Burial* (1963), pp. 131–39.

7 Quotations of the text of *Beowulf* are taken from *Beowulf and Judith*, ed. E. V. K. Dobbie, vol. IV of *The Anglo-Saxon Poetic Records* (1953).

Throughout this book in quoting Old English I have substituted *th* for the two unfamiliar letters used to represent that sound by the Anglo-Saxons.

Chapter II

1 Original text and discussion in R. W. Chambers, *Beowulf: An Introduction* (3rd ed., with a supplement by C. L. Wrenn, 1959), p. 305.

Chapter III

1 J. R. R. Tolkien, "*Beowulf*: The Monsters and the Critics," *Proceedings of the British Academy*, XXII (1936), 245–95; conveniently reprinted in *An Anthology of Beowulf Criticism*, ed. Lewis E. Nicholson (1963), pp. 51–103, and in *The Beowulf Poet*, ed. Donald K. Fry (1968), pp. 8–56.

2 C. S. Lewis, *A Preface to Paradise Lost* (1942), pp. 29–30.

INDEX

DATE DUE

OCT 1 9 71	FEB 1 1993		
AUG 6 '73			
	SEP 2 9 1993		
JAN 2 1974	DEC 0 7 1994		
OCT 1 2 1974			
	MAY 1 6 1995		
APR 4	FEB 0 1 1996		
	OCT 1 3 1995		
NOV 7			
	JUN 0 1 1996		
FEB 8	OCT 2 7 1996		
DEC 7 '79	NOV 0 7 1996		
SEP 2 1983	AUG 1 8 1997		
MAY 7 1985	APR 0 5 1998		
SEP 2 9 1986			
NOV 7 1986	FEB 0 1 2001		
SEP 2 5 1989	FEB 0 1 2001		
SEP 1 6 1991			
OCT 1 4 1991			

| | |